A Prayer Diary for Youth

BY

LEONARD P. BARNETT

THE METHODIST YOUTH DEPARTMENT
Ludgate Circus House, London, E.C. 4

THE EPWORTH PRESS
(FRANK H. CUMBERS)
23-35 City Road, London, E.C. 1

MELBOURNE   CAPE TOWN
NEW YORK   TORONTO

PRINTED AT THE CAMPFIELD PRESS, ST. ALBANS

PERSONALLY SPEAKING

PERSONALLY speaking, saying my prayers regularly is just about as difficult as anything in the whole Christian life. Quite often I'm not particularly aware of the presence of God. Equally often I don't feel any different afterwards from before. I'm ashamed many a time of the childish, repetitive phrases that well up from somewhere or other into the mind when trying to clothe my Godward thoughts with words. And there aren't many prayer-times that pass without the need for a strong rein on thoughts that will persist in rioting off along their own will-o'-the-wisp track.

That isn't all. I wish it were. What's still worse is the way in which I continually find to my cost how right the medieval Christians were to label Sloth as one of the Deadly Sins. Any Christian who is going to use prayer, in Dr. Leslie Weatherhead's telling phrase, as ' ten minutes a day for health's sake ', is going to have to fight for the opportunity, many a time. It's much easier not to. All of us find ourselves sometimes taking the easy way out. We're too tired, it's too late, we haven't left ourselves time. Sloth heaves a sluggish sigh of triumph and our prayers are left unsaid.

Worst of all is Pride, the pick of the whole bunch of Deadly Sins. Pride tells me that if normal Christians need daily prayer to keep them at concert pitch of Christian vitality, a clear-headed intelligent fellow like I am can easily afford to pray at intervals to suit himself. Anyway, Pride continues, prayer is an ' unpractical ' kind of pursuit. Those who pray a lot would probably be better off if they did more active Christian work such as I am so busy about.

Pride won't let me admit, without an effort, that prayer is both the noblest and the hardest activity men can attempt. Pride tries never to allow me to think that I am at fault when praying seems an impossibly difficult kind of exercise. Pride would forbid me to see how necessary an apprenticeship—mostly with dogged determination, occasionally with delight—one must serve in the school of prayer, before one experiences the joy of the master.

I know well however what the best Christians have said about prayer, right down the ages. They have all regarded prayer as the vital ingredient in the Christian's diet—the solid Bread of Life on which his soul is fed, and without which it dies. Their testimony is more than enough for me. If I flirt with Pride and Sloth, and allow myself to be deceived into thinking prayer doesn't matter, then I shall contract something that could be described as pernicious spiritual anaemia. If I persist in behaving so stupidly my spiritual experience will die.

This is not a matter of feeling. If it were, it wouldn't matter. Feelings seldom do, and never in the realm of prayer. This, however, is a matter of fact. If I am to climb sturdily as a Christian, then I must tread the path of prayer. Every proficient Christian has trodden the selfsame way. All bear the same testimony. But I find praying desperately hard work. I seem to hobble along at a painfully slow rate. Are there any crutches upon which I can lean from time to time, to help me tread a little firmer, a little faster?

Speaking personally, I can't be grateful enough for such crutches. And I'm encouraged to know that so many others have used them, too. Is there a Christian who at one time or another hasn't used the greatest passages from the Bible, and Christian hymnology, to help him express in sublime, timeless language, the aspirations of his heart? And are there not many other books of devotions one can use similarly? To one such book—Dr. John Baillie's *Diary of Private Prayer*—I shall forever remain outstandingly indebted. Those familiar with it will speedily discover how much it has influenced the presentation of the acts of devotion contained in this little book. And if through it, one other apprentice in prayer is helped as Dr. Baillie's book has helped me, it will have served its turn.

Here, obviously the richest parts by far are those in which I have introduced great Bible texts from both Old Testament and New: together with the use made of the hymns of Wesley and Watts, the greatest hymnwriters of all. As for the other prayers, I have prayed them should feel conscience-stricken who does not work steadily from the first day to the thirty-first, without let or hindrance.

Sometimes you may find a need to turn, with the help of the rather unusual Index at the back, to a different page from that which the calendar suggests. Then do so. The arrangement of the book is intended as a guide, not a chain.

On the other hand, don't rush to the other extreme, and open the pages at random day by day. Every page has at any rate been thought worthy of inclusion in the unity of the whole. Don't narrow the help all the pages together offer.

Above all, resist strenuously the temptation to use the Diary as though it were a normal book. It isn't. It's strictly within the ' apple a day ' category. Twenty apples in one day will fetch the doctor, not keep him away. Use this Diary equally foolishly and you will get spiritual indigestion, which can be a revolting experience, especially for those around you.

Where shall I pray?

By yourself is easily best—even if it means all sorts of dodges to contrive a time and place on your own. Unless you are a master, and not an apprentice, you need solitude in which to pray.

Don't be frightened of telling the folk you live with why you want some privacy. If they're amused, their amusement will soon turn into something very different. Stand by your guns! It's not nearly as difficult as you might think.

Last, I hope you'll want to read the Scripture passages in their full context. To do that, buy a Concordance if you haven't got one already. Then use it. It's one of the basic tools of the Christian trade.

L. P. B.

A Prayer Diary for Youth

O God, Thou art my God; early will I seek Thee.
Because Thy loving kindness is better than life my lips
shall praise Thee.
Because Thou hast been my help; therefore in the shadow
of Thy wings will I rejoice.

My Father, Thou hast caused again the darkness to give place to the light of a new day. Thou hast refreshed me in sleep. I praise Thee for a fit body and a ready mind with which to begin my work.

If I am to be taught, give me willingness to learn.
If my job bores me, give me patience with myself and charity towards others.
If I must do lowly or unpleasant tasks, give me the grace of cheerfulness.
If my work is strenuous, give me power to concentrate.
If it is quite beyond me, give me the courage to admit it.
If I find contentment and delight in my work, let me be grateful.
This day, Lord, help me to do the best I can.

I thank Thee that I shall go out into this day's life still surrounded by the unseen comradeship of family and friends; with a sense that we belong together, and to Thee. I thank Thee that I am not an outcast nor a stranger.
Let me be mindful, then, in this quiet moment, of those less fortunate than I am; the homeless; the workless, the imprisoned, the sick, and those who this day will die.

Christ, be Thou their strong Deliverer.

I remember in Thy presence my kinship also with millions of others who honour Thee and their fellows by their toil; in factories and fields, mines and offices, in the streets, in the air, on the seas. I depend upon them. We are members one of another. Without them I should not be warmed and fed, sheltered and clothed. My life, too, is part of Thy great scheme for the life of the world. Help me to see clearly what that part is, and to glorify Thee in all I say, and think, and do.

Let the words of my mouth and the meditation of my
heart be acceptable in Thy sight,
O Lord, my rock and my redeemer.

O Father, I thank Thee that though I often forgot
Thee this day, Thou didst hold me every moment in
Thy watchfulness and care. Now, at its ending, I
recollect this day's life. It was a gift from Thee, Father.
How did I use it?

Have I worked as though the eyes of Christ were upon
me?
For they were.
Have I talked as if Christ were the unseen listener?
For He was.
Have I behaved like an ambassador for Christ?
For I am.

Lord Jesus, I come to Thee this night to receive
Thy pardon and blessing. Forgive me, I pray, everything wherein I have hurt or disappointed Thee, wasted
my time, or misused my gifts. Forgive me all lack of
courtesy, hastiness in word and deed, meanness, spite,
and shirked witness.

Forgive me that as yet I have only partly learned to
let go of myself and cleave to Thee. I am sometimes
foolishly anxious and fearful about what folk say and
think of me. Help me more and more to know what
it means to abide in Thee, so that my thoughts become
Thy thoughts, my ways Thy ways. Give me such courage
and constancy that my witness by lip and life may be
equally yoked and plain to see.

And these prayers I ask for love of Thee and for Thy
sake Who didst die that I might live. Amen.

In the name of the Father, and the Son, and the Holy Spirit, I would both begin and continue this day. Amen.

God the Father, prevent me from this day denying in deed my brotherhood with all mankind.

From greed, sloth, pride, malice and impurity; O Father, deliver me.

God the Son, give me to find in my heart this day the compassion for my fellows which Thou didst continually show.

From impatience, contempt, prejudice, harshness, envy, and all lack of goodwill; O Christ, deliver me.

God the Holy Spirit, from Whom cometh every thought of goodness, grant me the desire continually to hear Thy still, small voice from within.

From self-deceit, self-will, stubbornness, vainglory, deafness of spirit; O Holy Spirit, deliver me.

Let me recollect what I plan to do this day . . . at home . . . at work . . . in my leisure time. . . .

O God, in all the busyness of this day, may I hallow Thy name.

Let me recollect and pray for the people I shall meet . . . especially................

O God, let my life and conversation be such as to glorify not me, but Thee.

Grant, O Loving Father, to all with whom I have to do, wellbeing in body, mind and spirit.

With Thee, O Father, I began this day. Grant me now,
at its ending, the sense of Thy nearness and the inner
royalty of Thy peace.

> *Now, O my God, Thou hast my soul,*
> *No longer mine, but Thine I am;*
> *Guard Thou Thine own, possess it whole,*
> *Cheer it with hope, with love inflame;*
> *Thou hast my spirit, there display*
> *Thy glory to the perfect day.*

I thank Thee, Lord:
  For the years in which I have enjoyed the countless
  blessings of my home. . . .
  For the delights of schooldays and holidays alike. . . .
  For health and strength. . . .
  For work to do. . . .
  For bright hopes. . . .

I pray Thee, Lord:
  For all now living bleak and comfortless lives:
  For those whose homes are destroyed:
  For those who live daily with hunger and destitution:
  For those without hope.

Especially would I remember before Thee all children
brought up in careless or unhappy homes, and prevented
there from ever truly seeing, as I have been taught to see,
what is good, and true, and beautiful; whose minds and
spirits have been stunted and warped; who look out on
life with dull or bitter eyes.

I pray for those who are deformed either in mind or
body; who cannot know the thrill of understanding difficult things, and making discoveries; who are denied the
excitement of playing a hard game, and exulting in the
pleasures of a body fit and whole; but who are
imprisoned, and have no hope of release. O God, Who
hast shown us in Jesus a compassion which is infinitely
tender and unceasingly active; teach me, I pray, so to
love Thee day by day as to find that same compassion
grow steadily in my heart. For Jesus' sake. Amen.

If I start this day with dull and sluggish spirit, then,
O God, quicken me with thoughts of Jesus:

> Who for years never shirked the labour of hard
> manual toil;
> Who sought not to evade the call to forsake family
> and friends;
> Who scorned ease, and suffered hardship;
> Who met misunderstanding, ingratitude, hatred with
> unyielding love;
> Who was in all points tempted like as I am, and was
> yet without sin.

Let me fortify my mind and heart upon the thought
that this same Jesus, the Man of Nazareth, is the eternal
Christ of God:

> Who was with God before the foundation of the world;
> Who is the living Word of God to man;
> Who is the Lord of all life;
> Who is the Redeemer of the world;
> Who is the Saviour of men;
> Who is the Head of the Church.

*O Jesus Christ, I lift my heart to Thee. Thou art my
Lord and my God. I pray Thee to keep me in Thy
power through every waking moment of this day.*

> *Take my soul and body's powers;*
> *Take my mind and memory, will,*
> *All my goods, and all my hours,*
> *All I know, and all I feel,*
> *All I think, or speak, or do;*
> *Take my heart, but make it new.*

I pray for all my fellow-Christians all over the world;
especially in lands where it is a dangerous thing to be a
Christian. May that vision of Thee, O Christ, Who art
alone able to keep us from falling, be ever bright and
clear; that in the evil day, Thy disciples may be found
faithful even unto death. I pray for my friends who
are committed Christians, especially for...............and
.... I thank Thee for older friends at my Church
and elsewhere, who have gone so much farther along the
Christian way, and whose example first turned my
thoughts to Thee; especially...............and...............
Lord grant that this day I may dishonour neither them
nor Thee. For Thy Name's sake. Amen.

*Lord, who shall sojourn in thy tabernacle? who shall
dwell in thy holy hill?*
*He that walketh uprightly, and worketh righteousness,
and speaketh truth in his heart.*
*He that slandereth not with his tongue, nor doeth evil
to his friend, nor taketh up a reproach against his
neighbour.*

Jesus said, I am the Truth.

O God, my Father, as I come to Thee for Thy
benediction upon this day's life, I pray Thee to bring
me out of the world of lies and half-truths into the
Light of Thy truth: that I may see myself, and the
world in which Thou hast put me, as they really are.
I need the surgery of Thy clean and Holy Spirit, to
cut out of my life those sins with which Thou alone
canst deal. Help me then to turn resolutely from the
voice of temptation, telling me

That my proneness to sin is part of my human inheritance, and that I can never hope for real change;
That my sins are as much other people's fault as
mine, and that I should not sin unless they provoked
me;
That others are as bad if not worse, and that it is
foolish to be over concerned;
That unless I sin, I can have no knowledge or experience of ' the world ';
That it is silly to aim too high;
That Thou wilt forgive me anyway.

*Help me to nail these lies in my own mind and heart,
Father, and to see them in all their falsity; for the sake
of Jesus Christ. Amen.*

I pray this night for all who have made shipwreck
of their lives through their own folly, or the folly of
others before them; for those who are striving to accept
the truth as it is in Jesus; for those who are finding
the Christian life strangely difficult, and tempted to step
aside out of the Way.

Lord, I am sometimes of their number and always I
am part of Thy Church. Grant that I may never grow
weary in well-doing, nor faint-hearted because others are
no better than I am.

I can do all things this day through Christ which
strengtheneth me.

> *O God, what offering shall I give*
> *   To Thee, the Lord of earth and skies?*
> *My spirit, soul, and flesh receive,*
> *   A holy, living sacrifice :*
> *Small as it is, 'tis all my store;*
> *More should'st Thou have, if I had more.*
>
> *Lord, arm me with Thy Spirit's might,*
> *   Since I am called by Thy great name;*
> *In Thee, let all my thoughts unite,*
> *   Of all my works be Thou the aim :*
> *Thy love attend me all my days,*
> *And my sole business be Thy praise.*

O God, I thank Thee:

For the clear morning light.

For the simple blessings of neat clothes and good food.

For the certainty of work to do, and a place that is
mine.

For the chance and challenge of this fresh, unspoiled
day.

Father, at the beginning of this day, I would quietly
recollect in Thy presence my aims and purposes.

I wish to get on, to be a success.

I wish to be well thought of, to earn the good esteem
of others.

I wish to become................

In these my desires, O God, may I never seek easy,
unworthy short cuts to success or personal popularity.
Help me to stand firmly by my principles, which are
founded on Thy truth. Help me to avoid riding rough-
shod over the rights and feelings of others. Give me
grace to deal courteously with difficult people. Help me
to withstand all temptation to scorn or irritation when
people disagree with me, or point out my weaknesses.
Help me to admit sensibly and swiftly when I am wrong.
Let me witness a good confession.

I remember before Thee all with whom this day I
shall have to do. . . .

I pray the divine light of Thy wisdom to illumine
those who confuse true success with ' getting on in life ';
remembering my own subtle temptations in this matter,
and how hard I find it to see at times that ' doing well '
may be different from ' living well '.

At the close of the day, I would receive the refreshment of God's presence and peace as I remember the words of Jesus.

Let your light so shine before men, that they may see your good works and glorify your Father which is in heaven.
O Jesus Christ, help me to obey this Thy word.
Love your enemies, and pray for them that persecute you.
O Jesus Christ, help me to obey this Thy word.
Seek ye first His kingdom, and His righteousness.
O Jesus Christ, help me to obey this Thy word.
Judge not, that ye be not judged.
O Jesus Christ, help me to obey this Thy word.
If thy brother sin against thee, go, show him his fault between thee and him alone.
O Jesus Christ, help me to obey this Thy word.
Whosoever would be first among you shall be your servant.
O Jesus Christ, help me to obey this Thy word.
When thou doest alms, let not thy left hand know what thy right hand doeth.
O Jesus Christ, help me to obey this Thy word.
Thou shalt love the Lord thy God with all thy heart, and with all thy soul, and with all thy mind, and with all thy strength.
O Jesus Christ, help me to obey this Thy word.
A new commandment give I unto you, that ye love one another; even as I have loved you, that ye also love one another.
If ye love me, ye will keep my commandments.

O God, I confess with shame that I so often love to obey the promptings of my own heart rather than the will of Christ. Stir up in me, and in all those who profess Thy holy name, an ever-stronger love for Thee, from which all ready obedience springs.

Unto Thee, O Lord, will I call; my rock, be not thou deaf unto me : lest, if thou be silent unto me, I become like them that go down into the pit.

Let me bring my doubts to mind. Sometimes I am tempted to doubt whether or not God exists. Sometimes I find it hard to believe that the Creator of the Universe can be my heavenly Father, who loves me and all mankind with an infinite love. At other times, my belief in Christ the Son of God is challenged, as to how God can ever be thought to have come to earth. And sometimes I cannot be sure of.............. Let me be sure of this :

> That all my doubts, and many more, have been faced by others, who have won through to the certainty of faith.
> That I should not be free to believe, unless I was equally free to doubt.
> That to doubt is not to sin.

Help me then, good Lord, to feel no false shame about my doubts. But let me face them sensibly and humbly. Give clarity and a sense of proportion to my kind. Let me ask :

> Do I ever use my doubts as a screen, to hide from the challenge of Christ to goodness and purity?
> Do I ever feel a sense of pride in airing my doubts, to make people think I am deeper than I am?
> Do I find time to read what stronger Christians than I have written to build up my faith and meet the questionings of my mind?
> Do I use my doubts as excuses for inaction?
> Do I clearly see that first, Christ says 'Follow Me'? And that afterwards, given my willing desire to follow, comes the task of fortifying my mind and heart upon the faith of a Christian?

I would not be a fool, saying in my heart, There is no God. Rather would I be wise with the wisdom Thy truth alone canst impart. Show me then, O Lord, Thy truth, and let me make it mine forever.

Teach me to use my doubts, not as frightening obstacles, but stepping stones across the floods of unbelief.

*Yea, though I walk through the valley of the shadow
of death, I will fear no evil; for Thou art with me.
The Lord is my light and my salvation; whom shall I
fear? The Lord is the strength of my life; of whom shall
I be afraid?
He that dwelleth in the secret place of the most High;
shall abide under the shadow of the Almighty. I will
say of the Lord, He is my refuge and my fortress; my
God, in whom I trust.*

I remember that fear is part of Thy wise design for
human life. Help me therefore to fear only those things
of which I ought, as Thy child, to stand in dread; and
for the rest, to garrison my heart with the power and
presence at all times of my Lord Christ.

Help me then, O God, by that same power, to put away
the fears of childhood:
  Fear of being alone, and of the dark;
  Fear of doing distasteful things, and hurting myself;
  Fear of strangers, going to fresh places, meeting people;
  doing unfamiliar things;
  Fear of failure.
Teach me rather, O God, to fear
  Compromising with the truth by silence or speech;
  Losing what good name I have;
  Bringing hurt or shame upon my family and friends;
  Breaking my word;
  Betraying Christ.

The fear of the Lord is clean, enduring for ever.

Bring me ever to remembrance, Lord, of the truth in
this matter—that I have no one to fear but Thyself.
Thou art the Judge of what is good and right. Teach me
fearlessly to disregard the opinions of others in those
things wherein they contradict the truth as I have learned
it of Christ.

Grant Thy succour to all this day who are in the grip
of fear, and who have no hold upon Thee. Raise up
those who are threatened with evil because of their faith
in Thee, who are being tested as by fire. May they find
in Thee their refuge and fortress, a very present help in
trouble and a deliverer from their fears. For the sake
of Jesus Christ, their Lord and mine. Amen.

Eternal Father, I begin this day with Thee. As I say my morning prayer, may I become very aware of Thy presence, Thy goodness, Thy truth. May I feel again the kindling of fresh desire to live this day for Christ.

Jesus said : Blessed is he, whosoever shall not be offended in me.

O Jesus Christ, I recollect Thy matchless goodwill to all people. Needy folk found in Thee a friend more steadfast than a brother. Unhappy people found Thy presence a benediction. Those without hope found in Thee new hope. Weak, wayward and sinful people found salvation in Thy words.

But those disfigured by the mask of self-righteousness and pride found Thy love and lowliness of heart, Thy purity and utter truthfulness, rising up as a shameful offence.

For all my good intentions, I recognise how easily I slip into their ranks. I tend to be secretly a little proud of my own virtue, thankful that I am not as the spiv.

In my heart of hearts, I yield to the temptation to be disgusted, not with sin, but with the sinners. Yet who am I to feel so? I, who often enough am guilty of the hurtful word, the tainted thought, the act of thought-lessness. I, who all too often am little-minded, priggish, jealous, greedy, mean.

Let me turn in true repentance to Christ.

When I survey the wondrous Cross
    On which the Prince of Glory died,
My richest gain I count but loss,
    And pour contempt on all my pride.

Forbid it, Lord, that I should boast,
    Save in the death of Christ, my God :
All the vain things that charm me most,
    I sacrifice them to His blood.

See, from His head, His hands, His feet,
    Sorrow and love flow mingled down :
Did e'er such love and sorrow meet,
    Or thorns compose so rich a crown?

Were the whole realm of nature mine,
    That were an offering far too small;
Love so amazing, so divine,
    Demands my soul, my life, my all.

O God, from whom cometh every good and perfect gift, I thank Thee for the priceless gift of worship.

Let me call to mind the privilege God has bestowed upon me of being part of the Church of Christ: a living Body, the great company of redeemed people spread abroad throughout the whole earth.

For my kinship with Christian people in every age and place; for the help and encouragement given me from them; for the intimate, strengthening fellowship of friends at church;
O God, I thank Thee.

For the immense privilege of Sunday worship; for times when I went to church spiritually dull and heavy, and came away with lightened mind and quickened spirit, restored to health again;
O God, I thank Thee.

For the blessings of hymns and prayers which spoke clearly things I desired to say, but could never find words to express; for the reading of the true and living Word, and for sermons which proclaimed a Gospel which fired my heart and rekindled my love of Thee;
O God, I thank Thee.

For the opportunities to work and witness for Thee, which came to me only through the life of the Church;
O God, I thank Thee.

For the meeting of mind and spirit with others treading the same path of Christian experience, through the fellowship given me at my church; fellowship which steadied and empowered me to endure temptations which would have led me from the Way;
O God, I thank Thee.

O God, I thank Thee indeed for this high privilege which is mine, to share in the life of Thy universal Church throughout the world, in and through the worship, work and service of my local church. Grant, I pray, that I may never grow so blind or foolish as to belittle in my own mind or in the presence of others, this vast treasure Thou hast bestowed upon me, in permitting me to take my place in the company of Thy faithful people. For Christ's sake. Amen.

O Lord, thou hast searched me, and known me.

Thou knowest my downsitting and mine uprising, thou understandest my thought afar off.

Thou searchest out my path and my lying down, and art acquainted with all my ways.

For there is not a word in my tongue, but, lo, O Lord, thou knowest it altogether.

Thou hast beset me behind and before and laid thine hand upon me.

Such knowledge is too wonderful for me; it is high, I cannot attain unto it.

Whither shall I go from thy spirit? or whither shall I flee from thy presence?

If I ascend up into heaven, thou art there: if I make my bed in Sheol, behold, thou art there.

If I take the wings of the morning, and dwell in the uttermost parts of the sea;
Even there shall thy hand lead me, and thy right hand shall hold me.

If I say, Surely the darkness shall overwhelm me, and the light about me shall be night;
Even the darkness hideth not from thee, but the night shineth as the day: the darkness and the light are both alike to thee.

How precious also are thy thoughts unto me, O God! how great is the sum of them!

If I should count them, they are more in number than the sand: when I awake, I am still with thee.

Search me, O God, and know my heart: try me, and know my thoughts.

And see if there be any way of wickedness in me, and lead me in the way everlasting.

O God, this night I come to my prayers with the unhappy
memory of disappointment fresh in my mind. I confess
my weakness and my need of comfort. I seek to stay
myself upon Thee before I sleep. Therefore would I not
forget Thy benefits, but remember that Thou art a God

    Who forgiveth all my iniquities;
    Who redeemeth my life from destruction;
    Who crowneth me with tender mercies;
    Who satisfieth my mouth with good things;
So that my youth is renewed like the eagle.

    Let me bring my disappointment into the presence of
the Heavenly Father.

Did I bring it upon myself?
*Then let me pray for grace to acknowledge that fact
to myself, and, if others too have been hurt, to make
amends.*
Did others cause it?
*Then let me pray for God's grace to put away all
bitterness of spirit.*
Did cherished hopes and plans go awry?
*Then let me pray for the renewed hope that God can
assuredly bring, and for a sense of proportion, lest I
be guilty of cherishing too much things which are of
little real importance.*
Was it a matter of personal failure?
*Then let me pray for grace to open my eyes to the
facts about myself that my disappointment has brought
me; and for grace to be guided by them.*

O God, I would remember, as I pray, my Lord Jesus.

I recollect how often He must have been tempted to
despair, and how sorely He must have needed the comfort
which now I seek of Thee. I remember how He prayed,
even upon the Cross of shame, for those who nailed
Him to it...............
    In the light of the Cross, my distress seems all un-
worthy of a child of Thine. Yet am I thankful that
Thou dost completely understand my heart, and canst
bear with me in all my childishness.
    I would be strong with the strength of Jesus, so that
honest failures and disappointments no longer have the
power to hurt me, still less to turn me from the Way.
Help me to gain that strength, Lord, from dwelling
in Thee daily.

Let me fill my waking mind with the thought of Jesus, one of the young men of Nazareth, getting up to go to work in the carpenter's shop. Sometimes He must have arisen tired, as I do, after a late night. Sometimes He must have felt inclined, as I am, to scamp His work. He was tempted in all points like me, yet He was without sin. He glorified the Father with honest work, well done. So must I. It is not only my duty. It is my privilege.

O Son of God, I thank Thee that Thou didst grace this workaday world with Thy human skill, and found joy in Thy labour. Teach me to think of Thee when I am content to offer less than my best to those for whom I work. Help me to shun the attitude of those who regard their job simply as a means of getting money. Help me to put myself into my work. If I can get on without trampling over others, then grant that I may get as good a job as I am fit to do.

I pray this day for those who have high positions in the workaday world, that they may be conscious of their stewardship and responsibility:
And for all those who work under them, that they may give a fair day's work for a fair day's wage.
I remember also all trainees, students, apprentices; that they may master their training and enjoy it with patience and perseverance.
Give Thy grace, O Lord, this day to those who are in dead-end jobs; and to those who are out of work. Save them from becoming cynical and hopeless.
To those who earn a living in unworthy or degrading ways give the desire to seek and find something better.
I pray also for the people I shall work with this day, especially...............

Grant that in my work equally as in my life and conversation, I may be found a faithful witness to the truth of the Gospel, for the sake of my Lord Jesus Christ. Amen.

> *O Thou who camest from above*
>   *The pure celestial fire to impart,*
> *Kindle a flame of sacred love*
>   *On the mean altar of my heart!*

> *Jesus, confirm my heart's desire*
>   *To work, and speak, and think for Thee;*
> *Still let me guard the holy fire,*
>   *And still stir up Thy gift in me.*

Yet as I pray this prayer, O Father, I recall clearly, and with shame, the way in which I allow that holy fire to die down in my heart.

My readiness to resent criticism; my unreadiness to face the truth.

My reluctance to sacrifice time and money to Thee; my willingness to spend both on myself.

My love of praise; my fear of unpopularity.

My lax thoughts; my stubborn self-will.

My lack of self-discipline; my unforgiving judgments.

My secret sins.

O God, make speed to save me.

> *I hold Thee with a trembling hand,*
>   *But will not let Thee go,*
> *Till steadfastly by faith I stand*
>   *And all Thy goodness know.*

> *Jesus Thine all-victorious love*
>   *Shed in my heart abroad;*
> *Then shall my feet no longer rove,*
>   *Rooted and fixed in God.*

> *O that in me the sacred fire*
>   *Might now begin to glow,*
> *Burn up the dross of base desire,*
>   *And make the mountains flow!*

> *Refining Fire, go through my heart,*
>   *Illuminate my soul;*
> *Scatter Thy life through every part,*
>   *And sanctify the whole.*

The presence of God is about me. His almighty power
is available for me. Nothing can happen to me this day
without His knowledge, and only my faithlessness can
defeat His purposes for my life. I need not live in-
gloriously. I can enjoy victory over sin and selfishness
. . . if I truly desire it.

I pray, O Lord God, that to all those who believe
and call themselves Christians, may come this day a
renewed and deep love for Thee and Thy truth, revealed
in Christ Jesus. We are the children of Thy love, yet
so aware of self-love and pride fighting for the mastery.
   The battle is set again this day between the things
which are true, honourable, just, pure, lovely, of good
report; and falsehood, dishonour, injustice, impurity,
ugliness, evil-speaking.
   Help Thy people everywhere, O God, continually to
dwell upon those things which proceed from Thy heart
of goodness: and to withstand, by Thy power, all the
assaults of the adversary: that they may not fall under
the power of the sins which so easily beset us, but may
have the victory promised in Jesus Christ our Lord.

I pray:
   For those who have been defeated again and again,
   and are depressed by their failure to grow in grace;
   that Thou mayest open their eyes to see why they
   have failed.
   For those who are relying too much upon their feelings, and are bewildered because they do not experience a continually warmed heart; that they may learn
   to love Thee with their minds as well as their hearts,
   their wills as well as their feelings.
   For those whose committal to Thee has not gone deep;
   who are like seed planted in stony soil, shrivelling in
   the heat of daily temptations: that they may learn their
   need of Thy indwelling Spirit day by day.
   For those who are still trying to follow both Thy
   way and their own, and enjoy at the same time selfish
   pleasures and the joy of Christ; that they may see
   how foolishly they are destroying their own true
   happiness.

O Lord, how manifold are Thy works! in wisdom hast Thou made them all : the earth is full of Thy riches.
I will sing unto the Lord as long as I live : I will sing praise to my God while I have any being.
Let my meditation be sweet unto him : I will rejoice in the Lord.

For the contentment of work done, and healthy tiredness:
God be praised.
For the certainty of sleep and the re-creation it will bring;
God be praised.
For a fit body and a lively mind, and a spirit aware of Him:
God be praised.
For the precious gifts of sight and imagination, and the beauty of everyday things:
God be praised.
For the rapture of music, and the inspiration of singing voices:
God be praised.
For the sheer delight of craftsmanship, and the warmth of a friendly hand:
God be praised.
For the power and ability to satisfy hunger and thirst with wholesome food and drink:
God be praised.
For homely neighbourhood smells, and the lovely perfume of flowers:
God be praised.

O God, prevent me from growing so stale and dull that I lose sight of the wonder and wealth of Thy world. Teach me to find Thy goodness everywhere, and finding it, let me be continually thankful. In the sights and sounds and experiences of the everyday, help me to discover Thee at work, Who art the Creator and Sustainer of the whole world. Above all, grant me the grace to see Thy most divine handiwork in the lives of Christian people, showing forth Thy truth, Thy beauty, Thy goodness. And let me find springing to birth each day, an ever stronger faith in the Lord Jesus Christ, the Saviour of men. Amen.

O God, Thou hast plainly taught us in Jesus Christ that nothing is too trivial for Thy care. And so I would bring to Thee in this morning hour, the little things of daily experience which have power to distress me; and about which I find it hard to speak to anyone. I would face these things in Thy presence, remembering that Thou dost understand me through and through, and canst enable me so to lay hold of Thee as to defeat all which causes unhappiness.

I pray Thy help especially:
  When I am tongue-tied.
  When my tongue runs away with me.
  When clever people confuse me.
  When my ignorance of ordinary things is uncovered.
  When I am slow to understand what is required of me.
  When I have made a foolish mistake.
  When people embarrass me.

O God, help me to know for sure that what matters is that I do my best at all times. Grant that I may feel shame at sins, not because I am guilty of honest mistakes and ignorance. Help me not to take too seriously the humiliations which all people suffer from time to time; but rather to remember resolutely the lesson which each one brings. As I grow in knowledge and confidence, help me also to grow up in all things unto Him which is the Head, even Christ.

I pray this day:
  For all who suffer far more than I have ever done.
  For those who have lost their sight, and must learn new skills, and the art of gracious dependence upon others.
  For those who have lost arms or legs, and who can never know the joys of games and sport, as I know them.
  For all helplessly crippled people, whose gaiety and gallantry is a challenge to those about them.
  For those who are tragically children in mind though adult in body.

O God, grant the ceaseless comfort of Thy peace to all such folk, that in their afflictions, they may build their minds and hearts upon Thee, and take Thy strength upon them. For the sake of Jesus Christ my Lord. Amen.

Honour thy father and thy mother.

I bow my knees unto the Father, from Whom every family in heaven and on earth is named.

Let me slowly recollect the countless lovingkindnesses I have received, down the years, from those who have made for me a home; a home in which I have been loved far beyond my deserving. As I remember, Lord, give me the grace of a truly thankful heart.

For mother . . . who risked her life to give me birth . . . who met my every need in infancy . . . who showed me first what love was . . . who shirked no tiresome or unpleasant task, that I might have comfort and wellbeing . . . who has given untold service to our home . . . whose steady loyalty is seen in a home where we enjoy cleanliness, good meals, and an ordered daily life . . . who continually takes our cares upon herself:

Lord, I am truly thankful.

For father . . . who has been her staunch partner down the years . . . whose daily work made it possible to bring our home into being . . . who has worked for us all as for himself . . . who could be gentle with my weaknesses and firm with folly . . . who taught me by his attitude to mother to set great store by consideration, courtesy, understanding, and doing as I would be done by:

Lord, I am truly thankful.

For both my father and mother, who proved to me the proper dignity and grace of manliness and womanhood, and how men and women can be true helps meet for each other; whose example has always made me think of the self-giving of God in Christ:

Lord, I am truly thankful.

O Father, who art the fount of all goodness and truth, I thank Thee for setting me in a family like mine, in which I have truly seen Thee at work, and in which I have learned so much of Thy way. Help me to be worthy of Thy goodness all my days. Amen.

O Heavenly Father, it is only a few hours since I stirred my heart to thankful remembrance of the blessings Thou hast so freely and continually given me through my home.

This day, therefore, I would ask Thee for grace to show my thankfulness not in word alone, but in deed; praying Thee most of all, in my dealings with those I love, to keep me from

Meanness and deceit:
Arrogance and self-conceit:
The contemptuous word:
Discourtesy and rude haste:
Moodiness and sulky behaviour:
Recklessness and impatience:
Failure in self-control.

Help me to see these things, O God, not as human failings, calling for no great concern, but as traitorous betrayals, evil in Thy sight, wounds in the body of our family life. Prevent me from being someone who takes great benefits with little thanks, who at home is treated best and behaves worst. Make me easy to live with, by the inflow of the spirit of Christ. Help me to cultivate the art of appreciation, quick to voice it, slow to criticise those who are doing their best. Save me from that hateful self-deception by which I can see no wrong in my own behaviour, and many faults in others. Help me to be a good neighbour to those who live nearest me.

I can do these things in Christ: and in Him only.

I pray:

For those who are far from home, and lonely:
For those who live in wrangling, disordered homes:
For those who treat their home as a lodging-house:
For those whose homes are broken:
For those who, even at home, are lonely:
For those who have no home.

O God, my Father, hear my prayer for all these Thy children. Succour them by Thy power. Lead them to see wherein they have failed themselves, their loved ones, and Thee. Grant them grace to desire the salvation from unhappiness and despair that Thou, in Christ, canst bring. For Thy Name's sake. Amen.

O Father Eternal, I thank Thee for the glorious certainty
of Thy gospel: and for all Thy people who have found
in Thee the unchanging rock upon which their lives were
built.   I thank Thee that there can be nothing happen
to me of chance and change, good or ill, to take me
from Thy presence both now and in the world to come.

I would pray Thee to help me make this prayer my
own.

> *Now I have found the ground wherein*
> *Sure my soul's anchor may remain—*
> *The wounds of Jesus, for my sin*
> *Before the world's foundation slain;*
> *Whose mercy shall unshaken stay,*
> *When heaven and earth are fled away.*

> *O Love, Thou bottomless abyss,*
> *My sins are swallowed up in Thee!*
> *Covered is my unrighteousness,*
> *Nor spot of guilt remains on me,*
> *While Jesu's blood through earth and skies*
> *Mercy, free, boundless mercy! cries.*

> *Though waves and storms go o'er my head,*
> *Though strength, and health, and friends*
> *Though joys be withered all and dead, [be gone.*
> *Though every comfort be withdrawn,*
> *On this my steadfast soul relies—*
> *Father, Thy mercy never dies!*

> *Fixed on this ground will I remain,*
> *Though my heart fail and flesh decay;*
> *This anchor shall my soul sustain,*
> *When earth's foundations melt away :*
> *Mercy's full power I then shall prove,*
> *Loved with an everlasting love.*

If thou wouldst be perfect . . . come, follow me.

I begin a fresh day with God . . . remembering in His sight this fact, that always men and women have been possessed of a ceaseless urge to improve upon things. Always there is the next stage to be reached. Always there are the men and women who dedicate themselves to reach that next stage . . . in the worlds of medicine and surgery, radio and television, architecture, engineering, travel by land, sea and air.

> *There is always a far horizon.*
> *There is always a better way.*

And for everyman, there is always a better life to be lived; cleaner, stronger, finer than the life of yesterday. God has put it into the heart of man to be discontented with less than the best. Nothing less than perfection is the goal, when sin and selfishness shall have been utterly rooted out by the redeeming power of God's holy love.

Am I aware of this, day by day?
Am I pressing on towards the goal unto the prize of the high calling of God in Christ Jesus?

> *What is our calling's glorious hope*
> *But inward holiness?*
> *For this to Jesus I look up,*
> *I calmly wait for this.*
>
> *I wait, till He shall touch me clean,*
> *Shall life and power impart,*
> *Give me that faith that casts out sin*
> *And purifies the heart.*
>
> *When Jesus makes my heart His home,*
> *My sin shall all depart;*
> *And lo, He saith : I quickly come,*
> *To fill and rule thy heart.*
>
> *Be it according to Thy word!*
> *Redeem me from all sin;*
> *My heart would now receive Thee, Lord,*
> *Come in, my Lord, come in!*

I began this day by recalling the life of victory over sin to which I am called; the more abundant life in the power of Jesus Christ; the life of perfect love.

At the closing of the day, I remember what I have done with it.

Have I worked as well as I should have done. . . ?
Has my conversation been wholesome and untainted. . .?
Have I been fair-minded. . . ?
Have I been a friend to all. . . ?
What have I done to prove my discipleship. . . ?

Lord, for every victory over the enemies that beset my body, mind and spirit, I am thankful.
Lord, for everything I am ashamed to remember, forgive me.

O Father, I would see clearly that this life of holiness to which Christ summons me, is not a life I must feverishly struggle to live in my own strength; but a life Thou dost offer me as a free gift, when my heart is truly set upon Thee. So often I try, and fail miserably, to do what I know I ought to do. I grow weary in well-doing, and despair of ever truly defeating sin within my life. Again I ask for the ability to understand the secret of saving faith in Jesus Christ; that faith which means a simple reliance upon Him whom Thou didst send to be a Saviour and a Friend to people like me, wayward and self-assured: faith to believe His promises and accept His deliverance.
Teach me O Father, that Christ indwells my life, that I may expressly show forth Thy love to others; that holiness is not holiness at all, which does not find its energy flowing out in service to others.

I pray Thy blessing this night upon all who in many ways fulfil Thy law of holy love: and especially. . . .
Those who care for homeless children:
Missionary doctors and nurses:
All preachers of the Gospel:
Sunday School teachers and youth workers:
Welfare workers, helping those in trouble:
Those who care for invalids, cripples and old folks;
All who pray for their fellow-men.

35

*O come, let us worship and bow down; let us kneel
before the Lord our Maker.
For he is our God, and we are the people of his pasture,
and the sheep of his hand.*

Then teach me, Good Shepherd, to accept the leading of
Thy hand, and not to fret because Thou dost sometimes
hold me back from the danger which I cannot see. If
my plan for this day meets with success, or failure, help
me to see Thy hand at work in everything, and glorify
Thee through good or ill.

Help me to worship Thee with my body as with my
spirit. It is Thy temple. Thy Holy Spirit seeks to
make it His dwelling. Keep my thoughts and actions
chaste, good Lord, through the self-control Thou alone
canst bestow upon me.

I would recognise in Thy sight that the life of the body
is Thy care; that Thou hast created within me those
very desires which so often I find perplexing and
troublesome.

Help me to see that through the life of the body, Thou
dost enable Thy children to share Thy highest work; the
making of new generations of people. Let me then
learn to look with awe and wonder upon the marvel of
Thy handiwork within me, and never to be guilty of
dishonouring this divine gift.

Yet even as I pray, O Lord, Thou knowest the quick
remembrances that flood my mind, of impure thoughts,
careless conversation, actions which have brought me
shame and remorse. I find it hard to win the victory
Thou hast promised me in this part of my life.

I am thankful that Thou dost perfectly understand me,
for Thou hast made me, and I am not tempted above that
which in Christ I am able to suffer.

O God, Thou hast made me for Thyself. Thou dost
understand me through and through. I thank Thee that
there is nothing at all within my life which is outside
the reach of Thy strong power. Then, Lord, when I
am weak and helpless, come to my rescue, and enable
me by faith in Thee, to win victories which seem
impossible.

Through the all-conquering might of Jesus Christ.
Amen.

Jesus said : Blessed are ye that weep now : for ye shall laugh.

Father of all goodness and wisdom, in knowledge of whom is my strength and salvation, I am thankful because sorrows and joys are joined together in the life of the world. I could not be happy if I never knew unhappiness. I could never know joy unless also I had encountered sorrow. I praise Thee because in Thy presence, joy and happiness are deepened, and sorrow is made bearable.

I would praise Thee for the simple delights which make life rich; and especially for the gift of pure and wholesome laughter.

I thank Thee :
For good jokes, honest wit, and happy absurdities :
For those gifted people who have the art of amusing others.

I pray Thee :
To help me appreciate wit, and shun malice :
To prevent me ever finding amusement in the humiliation of others or in their degradation.
To give me no part in heartless jests and indecent merriment.

Forbid it, Lord, that ever I should become so superficial and flippant as to treat life itself as a joke, withholding reverence from those things which are forever sacred. But save me, too, from stuffiness, the kind of solemn piety which repels people and makes them think that honest fun and true godliness are poles apart. I thank Thee that in this world, where through sin there is so much that is dark and cheerless, laughter can so often break through to lighten gloom and chase away the shadows for a while. But mostly do I offer my thanks for the true good news of Christ, the Bringer of joy, the Renewer of life and hope. I am glad because the Christian life is not one of grim and dull renunciation, but true self-fulfilment, and deepest joy.

I would remember now all those who are finding it very hard to capture the spirit of joy; the sick, in mind and body, and the sick at heart; the miserable, the lonely, the overworked, the anxious, the bereaved. In Thy mercy, lighten their darkness by the presence of Thy good Spirit.

For Jesus' sake. Amen.

Before the busy-ness of this day begins, let me be quiet, and hear God speak. Let me recollect His presence, His power, His purpose, for my life . . . this day.

I shall be tempted to live it as though no one really mattered but myself. Let me therefore remember the great family of mankind to which I am joined; praying for those in special need.

For people who will have to make decisions today, which will affect the rest of their lives, for good and ill:
O God hear my prayer.
For those who must stand trial in courts of justice: and for those who will stand in judgment on them:
O God hear my prayer.
For those who will receive bad news:
O God hear my prayer.
For women in childbirth and those who tend them:
O God hear my prayer.
For those who will be leaving home for the first time:
O God hear my prayer.
For those in peril by land, sea, and air:
O God hear my prayer.
For those sorely tempted to do great wrong:
O God hear my prayer.
For patients in hospital, and especially those undergoing operations:
O God hear my prayer.
For those who will be sitting for examinations:
O God hear my prayer.
For those who will be facing momentous interviews:
O God hear my prayer.
For those who will be starting their first job:
O God hear my prayer.
For those attending the funeral of a dear one:
O God hear my prayer.
For those who will face death:
O God hear my prayer.

Let me pray my own special prayers, for my friends . . . my companions throughout the day . . . for God's blessing upon whatsoever I shall do this day. . . .

O God, be Thou light and strength, courage and comfort, and peace that passeth understanding, to all for whom I have prayed; for Jesus Christ, His sake. Amen.

O Saviour Christ, as I rest my mind and spirit upon
Thee now, I would confess before Thee any ways in
which I have dishonoured Thy name and fallen short
of Thy will this day . . . confessing especially...............
I would offer no excuse. Thy presence was round about
me, yet I was blind to it, deaf to Thy voice. Renew
me, O Saviour. Cause me to find a perfect hatred
springing up in my heart of those words, thoughts, and
deeds which I know are an offence before Thee and a
betrayal of my discipleship. For Thy own sake. Amen.

From all unkind and doubtful conversation :
Christ, cleanse me.
From all lustful thoughts :
Christ, cleanse me.
From all snobbery and affectation :
Christ, cleanse me.
From all pride of place, and contempt :
Christ, cleanse me.
From all self-seeking and jealousy :
Christ, cleanse me.
From all meanness and malice :
Christ, cleanse me.
From all unworthy fear :
Christ, cleanse me.
From all bad temper and irritability :
Christ, cleanse me.
From all laziness :
Christ, cleanse me.

Help me to see these sins in their ugliness, O Lord.
And by Thy mercy, grant that their power over my life
may be broken, through faith in Thee. Amen.

I am grateful that Thou hast set me in a world where
so much that happens is a silent reminder of Thee.
I think of...............

The gay courage of many afflicted folk :
The warm encouragement of older people :
The unfailing patience of those tempted to ill temper :
The faith people have in each other.

O Jesus Christ, grant that I may not live either unobser-
vant or ungrateful. But let my life, catching goodness
from Thy divine goodness, shine with a Christlike radi-
ance to warm and strengthen others. And this once more
I ask in Thy name. Amen.

39

Gracious Father, Thou hast given many amazing gifts
to Thy children. I would be mindful of the priceless
treasure Thou hast bestowed in the Bible.

I would pause in awe and wonder to reflect upon
the miracle of God's Book. I call to mind...............

Those who, hundreds of years before the birth of
Christ, began to see the light of the Eternal breaking
upon them; who began to write of God's faithful dealings with His appointed people; who saw His handiwork
and sovereign power writ large upon the life of their
nation . . . and the nations about them . . . those who
wrestled with the facts of life, and death, judgment, and
suffering . . . of righteousness and justice . . . of mercy
and peace . . . of deliverance and salvation . . . who
slowly grasped with hands of faith, the message of a God
of compassion and love for all men . . . who set down
with an immortal pen, the truths divinely shown them.

Those who, when the Word was made flesh, remembered the words of Jesus . . . who wrote them down . . .
the story of the mighty acts of God in Christ, living,
dying, rising again . . . the Gospel writers who were
divine instruments to record the Passion of our Lord....

Those who set down the history of the infant Church
of Christ . . . who wrote letters which revealed still
more of the eternal truth of the Gospel . . . which made
plain the way of salvation through the grace of God,
by faith in His Son.

I would catch a vision of this great host of faithful
people, some known, many more unknown, by whose
obedience, insight, and unyielding labour I may know
the truths of God. Help me to dedicate the leisure
moments of my life this day, travelling or resting, in
conscious remembrance of the wonder of the Bible
record. And by that same Holy Spirit, stir up in me
the true desire to set forth by my life and conversation,
the same unending story of Thy goodness and truth.
Through Jesus Christ the Lord. Amen.

Again, Lord, I bring to mind the thoughts with which this day began.
Again would I offer my thanksgiving for Thy Book. And especially:

For those by whose devotion the early manuscripts of the Book were reverently guarded and transmitted:
For those who dedicated their lives to a fuller understanding of its pages:
For those who suffered torture, imprisonment and death, so that men might have free access to the Scriptures.
For the countless labours of men of scholarship, who have made it possible for ordinary people to read their Bibles with understanding and enlightenment:
For the enormous labours of faithful missionary scholars, who have translated the Bible into the tongue of a thousand peoples all over the earth:
For the work of the Bible Societies and all other agencies.

God's name be praised.

O God, I am ashamed, when I recall the faithfulness and devoted love of these my fellow Christians, that I know so little about the Book; that I am largely content to read it casually, vaguely, and without hunger in my heart for the truth it speaks. I should know enough of it to be able to speak plainly to others about it, to defend its truth, and to commend its message. Help me to confess this matter as a part of my discipleship which I have neglected. Let me feel shame to know so much more about magazines and newspapers than I do about the Bible. Give me to want to become a workman unashamed, handling aright the word of life. Amen.

Let me spend a minute in quiet reflection:

Have I ever systematically read and studied the Bible, giving even so little as an hour a week to it?
If not, why should I not do this?
Am I too lazy?
How deep does my loyalty to Christ go?

Christ, help me to turn my high intentions into deeds. Save me from empty promises and lifeless aspirations, for Thy Name's sake. Amen.

I will lift up mine eyes unto the mountains:
From whence shall my help come?
My help cometh from the Lord,
Which made heaven and earth.
He will not suffer thy foot to be moved:
He that keepeth thee will not slumber.
Behold, He that keepeth Israel shall neither slumber nor sleep.
The Lord is thy keeper:
The Lord is thy shade upon thy right hand.
The sun shall not smite thee by day, nor the moon by night.
The Lord shall keep thee from all evil;
He shall keep thy soul.
The Lord shall keep thy going out and thy coming in, from this time forth and for evermore.

O Lord, my Helper, Thou hast called me to be a witness to the truth of the Gospel of Jesus Christ. I am called by His name, I stand in His stead. I am an ambassador for Christ.

Then, Lord, be very near to me this day, and guide me in all I say and do; that I may be saved from the blundering faults and sins which turn people away from Christian truth.

I pray in particular for those with whom I shall live and work this day. . . . I name them before Thee............

O Lord, Thou knowest how many of these my companions belong to Thee as committed followers of Christ. Thou knowest too how hard it is, so often, to see what I must do, and say, in order to be a faithful witness. Yet Thou art indeed my Helper and my Friend. As I rely in simple faith upon Thy word, so shall I learn from day to day what I must do to witness a good confession.

Save me, Lord:

From hesitation and timidity:
From over-confidence and a dictatorial manner:
From silence when I should speak out:
From words that should remain unsaid:
From allowing profession to stride ahead of practice:
From witnessing to a good conceit of myself instead of to Thy love and Thy glory.

Lord, I thank Thee for the restfulness of this evening hour. Today has been spent in a loud and clamorous world. I am thankful for the peace and quiet of this time and place. Now may I recollect my Heavenly Father, Whose invisible presence has shielded me throughout the day: whose ceaseless care brings on again the evening shadows and the promise of refreshing sleep. In His presence I would stay my spirit upon the unchanging truth of God, His wise and good design for my life. I would be strengthened in the inner man by renewed faith in Him.

> Come, Holy Ghost, all-quickening fire!
>   Come, and my hallowed heart inspire,
> Sprinkled with the atoning blood;
>   Now to my soul Thyself reveal,
> Thy mighty working let me feel,
>   And know that I am born of God.
>
> Humble, and teachable, and mild,
>   O may I, as a little child,
> My lowly Master's steps pursue!
>   Be anger to my soul unknown,
> Hate, envy, jealousy, be gone;
>   In love create Thou all things new.

O God, I pray for any this night who may think hard thoughts about me. For those whom I may have disappointed or aggrieved. . . . I pray also for those against whom I may be tempted to hold a grudge . . . that all unfriendliness and hostility may melt away from my heart in the light of this Thy presence.

I would pray too for those whose hearts are consumed with hatred, envy, jealousy; for everyone whose mind and heart is torn with violent evil. O God, no cure can be brought for such diseased folk apart from Thine almighty power. Speak, then, through Thy servants, that those who lie this night with distressed and distorted minds, through sin, may come to the blessed knowledge of Jesus Christ the Saviour from sin, and may know the forgiveness, love and peace which are the healthful gifts of His salvation.

43

Lord Jesus, for Thy humble heart, Thy gracious spirit,
Thy boundless goodwill, I ask Thee now.

To meet merited rebukes without rancour:
Christ, enable me.

To meet difficulties with cheerfulness:
Christ, enable me.

To be glad when others succeed, even where I fail:
Christ, enable me.

To resist self-pity:
Christ, enable me.

To avoid conceit and arrogance, giving respect where
it is due:
Christ, enable me.

To be chaste, in thought, word and deed:
Christ, enable me.

To be obedient to those in authority:
Christ, enable me.

These blessings, O Saviour, I beseech not only for
myself but for all Thy people; especially those who are
finding life hard and unpromising: those who are
possessed of nagging fears and anxieties; and those who
must spend today in the company of unsympathetic and
cynical companions.

> *I want Thy life, Thy purity,*
> *Thy righteousness brought in;*
> *I ask, desire, and trust in Thee,*
> *To be redeemed from sin.*
>
> *Anger and sloth, desire and pride,*
> *This moment be subdued;*
> *Be cast into the crimson tide*
> *Of my Redeemer's blood!*
>
> *Saviour, to Thee my soul looks up.*
> *My present Saviour Thou!*
> *In all the confidence and hope,*
> *I claim the blessing now.*

May that blessing belong to all those who are called
to do great things for Thee today. That Thy will may
be done, and Thy blessed Kingdom brought nearer.
Amen.

God calls me to live as a citizen of His Heavenly Kingdom. Yet I must prove that citizenship in the life of
my neighbourhood. Christians are the leaven in the
lump, working within it to transform the whole. I take
my place as a co-worker with God, as a brother to all
men, as the herald of good news. It is my privilege to
work and pray for the happiness and wellbeing of the
community of which I form part. I am thankful, O
Father, for the inspiration of the storied past, and those
who have served the common good, making the life of
our nation what it is today. . . .

For statesmen who hammered out on the anvil of history the principles of law and order, justice, and the
democratic government of our land.
For those who in many ages have died to gain and
keep the freedom we are privileged to enjoy. . . .
For adventurous travellers who broadened our horizons, and enriched our common heritage. . . .
For scientists who wrested the untold secrets of nature,
and whose discoveries and inventions have changed the
lives of succeeding ages, placing marvels within our
hands to make life inexhaustibly varied and engrossing.
For scholars, writers, painters, musicians, who have
added so enormously to our common store of beauty,
delight and understanding: without whom the life of
our nation would have been poor indeed. . . .

O Lord, I would not live regardless of these Thy children, my fellow-countrymen, who fought with hand and
brain and spirit to secure a fuller life for others.
Help me to serve the present age with the constancy,
devotion, and self-sacrifice which these great and famous
ones of old displayed; since I am called by Thy name,
and enjoy the unending wealth of Thy labour, and theirs,
as co-workers with Thee.
I pray for my country: for all who hold positions of
great power and authority, that they may not be cor-
rupted by that power, but remain aware of their stewardship. I pray for those who hold responsibility great and
small in town and countryside throughout this land; that
they may be supported and encouraged in all that is wise
and good, and over-ruled in all things out of harmony
with Thy good will. Through Jesus Christ, my Lord.
Amen.

Before I go about the business of this day, warmed, fed, clothed, and with friendly faces around me, I would pray for those to whom these many blessings have been denied.

Hear my prayer, O Father:

For those who live in huts and hovels, with no place to call a home: the refugees and wanderers over the face of the earth:

For those who are starving, especially little children and old people, so helpless and dependent upon the strength and kindness of others:

For those who live in homes of filth and squalor, where no comfort or love dwells, and evil reigns:

For those who live on their own, keeping themselves apart from their fellows, and know nothing of the lively joy of friends and home life: and those who are forced so to live, and are unbearably lonely:

For those who live as strangers in a strange land, far from their fellow-countrymen, and who feel at times a dreadful sense of isolation and loss.

Loving Father, I would not live this day unmindful of these my brothers and sisters. Help me to live as I pray, so that if it is given me today to stretch out the hand of sympathy and friendliness, no stupid bashfulness or undue timidity may cause me to turn away before my Christian task is done.

Especially do I pray for all those who suffer the pain of mind and body, and the loss of those blessings which are theirs by right, through the sin and carelessness of other people. I remember deprived boys and girls, those who have been forced to live away from their own parents; that those into whose care they have been given may make up by their own encouraging love, for the loss such children have suffered.

I pray too for young people in Approved Schools, prisons, and other such places. O God, prevent me from the loathsome sin of thinking myself better far than such people, but rather let me see them through Thy eyes. I pray especially for all older people set in authority in such schools and reformatories, that in all they do and say, they may be upheld and guided by Thy Holy Spirit, Who is able to redeem to the uttermost all that call upon Thee.

Lord, I confess again with shame this night how hard I find it to keep my soul and body chaste. I find myself overtaken in sins of the mind almost before I am aware of the temptation. I find within me imperious desires which tend all too often to defeat me. I know full well Thou alone canst enable me to harness and control them. I am encouraged to remember how many of Thy saints have been sorely troubled even as I am; and how they have won through to purity of mind and life by the working of Thy good Spirit. Teach me how to overcome despondency and fruitless self-reproach. Help me to turn remorse into repentance. Remind me again that the gift of physical impulse and desire is part of Thy plan for human life; and that if I am both patient and faithful, Thou wilt enable me to use this great and divine gift to Thy glory and the fulfilment of Thy design for my life.
Through Jesus Christ my Lord. Amen.

> *All things are possible to him*
> *That can in Jesu's name believe:*
> *Lord, I no more Thy truth blaspheme,*
> *Thy truth I lovingly receive;*
> *I can, I do believe in Thee,*
> *All things are possible to me.*

I pray now for all those who are overtaken with strong temptation, and ready to cease from battle, and to lay down their arms. Help them to resist the voice of the tempter, but to fight a good fight, and to finish the course. Remind them as I pray Thee to remind me, that theirs is the gift of the shield of faith, the helmet of salvation, the sword of Thy Spirit, the living word of God. Help them truly to gird their loins with truth, and to clothe their body with the breastplate of righteousness; that not all the fiery darts of the evil one may be able to penetrate their Christian armour. Amen.

Therefore, let us also, seeing we are encompassed about with so great a cloud of witnesses, lay aside every weight, and the sin which doth so easily beset us, and let us run with patience the race that is set before us, looking unto Jesus, the author and perfecter of our faith, who for the joy that was set before Him endured the cross, despising shame, and hath sat down at the right hand of the throne of God.

At the start of this day, I think of the tasks I shall be set to do. They will either be my means of livelihood, or they will help to prepare me for the responsibility later on of earning a living. Whether the one or the other, I have my work to do today. God be praised that I am not condemned to idleness, hurtful alike to mind and body of those able and willing to work but who can find no one wanting them. Let me pray with compassion in my heart for all unemployed people, hoping against hope, battling against despair and bitterness, distress and ill-health.

O Son of God, the carpenter, I thank Thee that Thou wast a workman, with aching muscles and sweaty body at the end of the day; that Thou didst grace this worka-day world with Thy human skill, and found joy in Thy labour. Teach me at all times to think on Thee when-ever I find myself growing content with less than my best, and prone to scamp the jobs I am set to do.

Teach me to rejoice in hard work that stretches mind or sinew to the full. Give me such a mind to work that I may ever despise a slipshod attitude to my task.

Help me to be co-operative. Help me to shun the atti-tude of those who regard their job simply as a means of getting money. Help me to put myself into my work.

I pray O Lord:

For all whose typewriter is the tool of their craft.
For those who drive vehicles by road and rail, and those who service them.
For all airmen and seamen.
For those who mind machines.
For those who work in gardens and with all growing things.
For all who serve the public in shops and offices.
For all ministers of the Gospel . . . especially my own minister...............
For teachers of every kind, and their pupils; especially...............and...............
For those who guard our health—doctors, hospital staffs, dustbin men, sewerage workers.
For miners.
For police officers, and those who administer the law.
For...............and...............and...............
Hallowed be Thy Name, in their labour, this day and always. Amen.

Let me, in the presence of God, this night, look quietly at the pleasures I seek, reminding myself that pleasures are good or bad as I make them so.

Do I take pleasure:
In good books, newspapers and magazines?
In films, plays, radio and television programmes?
In sports and spectacle?
In witty conversation and good humour?
In music, singing and dancing?
In good food?
In arts and crafts?
In home comforts and gardens?
In birds and animals?
In the glory of fields and woods, mountains, rivers, and sea and sky?

God be praised, Who hast made the earth so full of wonder and delight, and Who has so made me that I find pleasure in such things. Save me from spurning any of them through a false sense of superiority. Give me the grace to take my pleasures with temperance and yet keen enjoyment; that I may never confuse pleasure with happiness, nor think that my pleasures can ever yield me the deep joy that only comes from living up-rightly, generously, honestly, caring more for others' well-being than my own personal satisfactions.

Give me to know, Lord, whenever my love of pleasures threatens my love for Thee, that I may not fall into grievous sin by setting more store upon Thy creatures than upon their Creator. Help me too to know whenever my pleasures tend to become unwholesome or tainted; that I may have in such moments the mind of Christ, to withstand the sins that can so easily beset me.

O God I pray Thy blessing upon all those whose out-standing gifts of hand and eye and brain are used to unfold to their fellow-men the wonder and the wealth of thy world. Those who speak, and write, paint and compose, fashion and create things of beauty, worth and insight, which reveal Thy nature.

Let me not grow fretful as I remember how little are my own talents. But rather teach me how brilliant a disciple of Christ I may become as I seek always to serve all those around me with true humility and constant goodwill.

O God, I thank Thee for the insight and understanding of the apostle Paul, who declared the eternal truths of the Christian Gospel in words I must strive to understand.

When I am tempted to think that obedience to good rules of conduct can put me right with God; when I am tempted to believe men can after all manufacture their own deliverance from sin and selfishness, help me to grasp the inward and eternal truth of this Thy word, as proclaimed by Thine apostle.

For all have sinned, and fall short of the glory of God; Being justified freely by his grace through the redemption that is in Christ Jesus:

Whom God set forth to be a propitiation, through faith, by his blood, to shew his righteousness, because of the passing over of the sins done aforetime, in the forbearance of God;

Being therefore justified by faith, let us have peace with God through our Lord Jesus Christ;

Through whom also we have had our access by faith into this grace wherein we stand; and let us rejoice in hope of the glory of God.

There is therefore now no condemnation to them that are in Christ Jesus.

For the law of the Spirit of life in Christ Jesus made me free from the law of sin and of death.

What then shall we say to these things? If God is for us, who is against us?

He that spared not his own Son, but delivered him up for us all, how shall he not also with him freely give us all things?

Who shall separate us from the love of Christ? shall tribulation, or anguish, or persecution, or famine, or nakedness, or peril, or sword?

Nay, in all these things we are more than conquerors through him that loved us.

For I am persuaded that neither death, nor life, nor angels, nor principalities, nor things present, nor things to come, nor powers, nor height, nor depth, nor any other creature, shall be able to separate us from the love of God, which is in Christ Jesus our Lord.

Lord, if I but dimly comprehend the glorious truth of this Thy Gospel, help me to think and pray and worship until Thy Holy Spirit shall make all things clear to me. Amen.

As I come to my prayer time I am out of sorts and unhappy, smarting still from the remembrance of the things which have happened to me today. I do not feel at all like saying my prayers.

Then let me not try to say anything. Let me try to be quiet, to take my mind off myself, and allow God to speak to me. . . . Let me put my thoughts consciously upon other people, with the desire in my mind that some-how, because I have remembered them before God, they may be blessed by Him. . . . Those who, even at this very moment, are fighting for life . . . the desperately ill, those who have been injured this day by accident in fac-tories, fields, on the streets . . . especially tiny children and old people . . . and the devoted nurses who will watch over them while I take my rest. . . .

The dear ones and friends of such victims, to whom this day has brought shock and distress . . . who even now are anxiously waiting for fresh news . . . some of them hoping against hope . . . all feeling a sense of desolation and helplessness. . . . My own doctor, whose telephone may even now be calling him out to relieve someone's pain and anxiety. . . . Anybody I know who is now or who has recently been in trouble of any kind. . . .

Those who today have been sent to prison, or away from home because of wrong-doing, for the first time. . . . Those who are spending their first night away from home, in the Forces or elsewhere. . . .

O God, in Thy mercy, grant the grace of courage and true wisdom to all such. For Jesus' sake. Amen.

And now, let me join with the great company of my fellow-Christians, down the ages even until now, who have made this prayer their own.

O Saviour of the world, the Son, Lord Jesus :
Stir up Thy strength and help us, we humbly beseech Thee.
By Thy Cross and precious blood Thou hast redeemed us :
Save us and help us, we humbly beseech Thee.
Thou didst save Thy disciples when ready to perish :
Hear us and save us, we humbly beseech Thee.
Let the pitifulness of Thy great mercy : Loose us from our sins, we humbly beseech Thee. Amen.

God be praised for the dawn, fresh morning air, and
strength renewed; for the unspoiled challenge of a new
day, and work to be done.

What was it that spoiled yesterday for me?

Did someone make me annoyed by speaking the truth
without wrapping it up in smooth words?
Did I play the fool, and then resent the merited rebuke?
Did I fail to get my own way, and then sulk?
Did someone catch me on the raw?
Did I give way to some sin I had forsworn, and so
was disgusted with myself?

Was it my fault? Even partly?

Then let me ask God's forgiveness slowly and
deliberately, neither wallowing in my sense of wrong-
doing nor glossing lightly over it.
Is there anything to be done to set things aright?
Ought I to apologise to someone?
Ought I to make amends in some other way?

*Was it not my fault at all? Did it happen through
the selfishness of others?*

Then I must learn the hardest lesson of all—sin bearing.
I must shoulder the cross Jesus warned that each disciple
should find. He did not rebel against His cross, and
by it mine is the tiniest thing. He still loved the sinner
while hating his sin. So must I.
But Christ, this is too hard for me. I can with diffi-
culty tolerate those who treat me badly, but to feel
goodwill towards them is impossible. Yet what is impossible to me is possible to Thee.
Cast out of me, Saviour, all bitterness and hatred.
Give me grace to pray this prayer: Father, forgive my
trespasses, as I forgive them that trespass against me.

Was it no one's fault? Was it a sheer accident?

Then let me treat it as such, and not try to assume
even for a moment that someone—not myself—is to
blame. Help me to see the matter straight. Save me
from the sin of treating something unimportant as though
it was a matter of life and death. Let me not give place
to self-pity. Help me to read the lesson Thou didst
have for me in what happened yesterday. And help me
to do better far today. For Christ's sake. Amen.

Wherewithal shall a young man cleanse his way? by taking heed thereto according to thy word.
With my whole heart have I sought thee : O let me not wander from thy commandments.

O God, I remember with thankfulness that Thy precepts are unchanging, sure and true. Thou art a God Who abides faithful, and in Whom there is no variation. I may come to Thee and steady myself upon Thee as upon an immovable rock. Grant me renewed wisdom, understanding, and the liberty that belongs to the children of God, as I worship Thee afresh.

I come to Thee very conscious that I am unlike Thee. I am inconstant. I break my word. I am unreliable and changeable. Sometimes I hardly recognise myself. I am not nearly the fine person I would like others often enough to think me.

From
    All my selfcentredness and sham :
    My hardness of heart with others, and indulgence with myself :
    My fads and fancies, and my changeability :
    Everything ugly in my life and character :
    O Saviour Christ, deliver me day by day.

I would pray especially this night for those who have most to do with me from day to day.
    My parents and guardians, who have known me longest and know me best; to whom I owe life and health and unnumbered gifts. . . . The people who live next door . . . our neighbours . . . who do not always perhaps find it easier to be happy because we live close by. . . . My friends at church . . . at school . . . college or work . . . who have stood by me so often and encouraged me . . . my friends whom, like my loved ones, I sometimes ignore. . . . The people I work with . . . and the people whose orders I must obey . . . some of whom find me as awkward as I find them . . . who have their own private difficulties to face . . . their own troubles and anxieties which I seldom even think about. . . .

O God, my Father, once more I would consecrate my life to Thee. Help me to be a better disciple as the days go by. Amen.

This day, no less than any other, will never come again. I cannot retrace a single step. For good or ill, my actions will abide. This day is the gift of God.

What do I plan to do?
Can I ask God's blessing on it all? Then let me do so now.

How do I generally spend my time?
During my working hours, do I give myself without stint to whatever work falls to me? Do I watch the clock?

How do I spend my leisure?
Do I live as a child of God, or a creature of appetite?

What time do I set aside regularly for:
Reading the Bible?
Saying my prayers?
Sharing fellowship with my fellow Christians?
Public worship?

How many hours each week do I devote to:
Going to the pictures, or the theatre?
Playing games?
Amusing myself in other ways?
Enjoying myself with my friends?

Do I see that time is kept regularly for:
My family?
Reading more about my faith?
Training myself for Christian witness?
Christian service of a definite character?

For everything which speaks of selfishness and self-indulgence, I ask Thy forgiveness, O God. Help me to live as redeeming the time. Quicken within me the desire to live this and every day as a child of the Heavenly Father, for Thy sake. Amen.

I pray in Christian love, for all those to whom the passing hours of this day will bring little respite from grief or pain; for those tormented with anxiety, and borne down with sorrow. O God, when all earthly helpers fail, Thou art the same everlasting God of mercy. Thou are the Physician of the mind and soul. Look with compassion upon these Thy children, and give them Thy peace. For the sake of Christ the Redeemer. Amen.

Jesus said: *Have faith in God.*

The apostle Paul said: *By grace have ye been saved through faith : and that not of yourselves : it is the gift of God.*

Another apostle said: *Now faith is the assurance of things hoped for, the proving of things not seen.*

O Lord, I am thankful because from the life of every-day, I may learn what faith is. I think of my dear ones, upon whose constant kindness and love I have learned to rely from my earliest days. I think of my friends, upon whom in like manner I can depend, and whose loyalty confirms continually the faith I have in them.

From my family and friends I have learned the reality of faith. I have learned how to put my whole trust in others.

O God, help me clearly to see how like this is the faith Thou dost bid us put in Thyself; that there is nothing of childish magic or superstition about it; still less is it a gift which is bestowed on some and denied to others, to have faith in Thee.

I thank Thee for the measure of faith Thou hast implanted in me thus far along the road of Christian experience.

For the faith I have that Thou hast made this limitless universe, and dost unceasingly exercise Thy controlling power over it: For the faith I enjoy that Thou art a God of goodness and truth, Who hast founded the life of mankind upon eternal, righteous laws, in obedience to which men may live well.

For the faith I cherish that Thou art not a God remote from the lives of Thy children; but hast revealed Thyself in many ways and through many gifted men and women, and in Jesus Christ Thine only begotten Son, Who with the Holy Spirit, liveth and reigneth with Thee, one God, eternally.

For the faith to which I cleave that the final victory will one day be with righteousness, and truth; and that evil must finally perish; the faith to believe that Thy kingly reign of love and peace shall be established over the whole earth:

I thank Thee, O God.

The Lord is my shepherd; I shall not want.
He maketh me to lie down in green pastures : he leadeth
me beside the still waters.
He restoreth my soul : he guideth me in the paths of
righteousness for his name's sake.
Yea, though I walk through the valley of the shadow
of death, I will fear no evil; for Thou art with me:
thy rod and thy staff, they comfort me.
Thou preparest a table before me in the presence of
mine enemies: thou hast anointed my head with oil; my
cup runneth over.
Surely goodness and mercy shall follow me all the days
of my life : and I will dwell in the house of the Lord
for ever.

O God, Thou great Shepherd of the sheep, once again
I thank Thee for the refreshment of mind and spirit
Thou hast provided along the path of daily life.

For the stimulus of Christian friends and fellowship in
which we are able to see clearly together the problems
and opportunities of Christian life and witness; the
meaning of the Bible and the task of the Church; the
lessons of the past, and plans for future days.

For the life-giving hours of public worship week by
week, when through the proclamation of Thy Gospel
by word and sacrament we are truly refreshed in the
presence of Thy life-giving Spirit. For the triumphant
and searching hymns of faith; for the immemorial words
of Scripture speaking again and again to our need.

For the stimulus of living day by day in an environ-
ment at most but partly Christian; in which I am challenged to evidence my faith, in life and conduct which
shall stamp me as a Christian.

For the vast encouragement of Christian literature of
so many kinds, through which my mind and heart are
sharpened again and again to discover fresh aspects of
Thy truth. For books about the Bible, books about
Christian experience, books about Christian belief, books
about great Christians; all of them building up the life
of the spirit in strength, vigour and maturity.

Jesus prayed:

*And now, O Father, glorify thou me with thine own
self with the glory which I had with thee before the
world was.*

*I manifested thy name unto the men whom thou gavest
me out of the world: thine they were, and thou gavest
them to me; and they have kept thy word.*

*And for their sakes I sanctify myself, that they themselves
also may be sanctified in truth.*

*Neither for these only do I pray, but for them also that
believe on me through their word;*

*That they may all be one; even as thou, Father, art in
me, and I in thee, that they also may be in us: that the
world may believe that thou didst send me.*

O God, grant that I may truly understand this prayer
of Jesus; that I, too, may share His longing that Christians
should be one.

As a follower of Christ and a member of the Christian
family, I do not join a united World Christian Church
which is His undivided Body. I join a Church which
is a fragment of the whole, a member of the Body
separated in large or small measure, from the other members. Yet would I recall that each of the members of
this broken Body have kept alive, through the Spirit
and direction of the Head, the Gospel committed to it.

And I would also recall the truly marvellous way in
which the Christ Who is the Head of the Church has led
the Churches of this and the last century to think again
about their nature and calling; so that many scores of
denominations have begun to establish fellowship together
to put in hand common Christian enterprises, to discover
an essential spiritual unity in Christian action and
experience.

I remember the national Councils of Churches which
have come into being in recent years and the great fact
of world fellowship and united Christian action within
the World Council of Churches.

O God, I praise Thee that I am living in an age when
men's hearts are turning again to the prayer of Jesus,
with longing that it might be realised. Grant, O God,
that I may do all that it is within my power to do, to
speed the day when there shall indeed be one fold, even
as Thou art the one Shepherd of us all. Amen.

The apostle Paul wrote:

I beseech you, therefore, brethren, by the mercies of God, to present your bodies a living sacrifice, holy, acceptable to God, which is your reasonable service.

And be not fashioned according to this world: but be ye transformed by the renewing of your mind, that ye may prove what is the good and acceptable and perfect will of God.

O God, help me gladly to receive and obey this Thy word.

Let love be without hypocrisy. Abhor that which is evil; cleave to that which is good.

Be of the same mind one toward another. Set not your mind on high things, but condescend to things that are lowly. Be not wise in your own conceits.

O God, help me gladly to receive and obey this Thy word.

But if thine enemy hunger, feed him; if he thirst, give him to drink: for in so doing thou shalt heap coals of fire upon his head.

O God, help me gladly to receive and obey this Thy word.

Bear ye one another's burdens, and so fulfil the law of Christ.

O God, help me gladly to receive and obey this Thy word.

Wherefore, putting away falsehood, speak ye truth each one with his neighbour: for we are members one of another.

Let all bitterness, and wrath, and anger, and clamour, and railing, be put away from you, with all malice:

And be ye kind, one to another, tenderhearted, forgiving each other, even as God also in Christ forgave you.

O God, help me gladly to receive and obey this Thy word.

Finally, be strong in the Lord, and in the strength of his might.

Put on the whole armour of God, that ye may be able to stand against the wiles of the devil.

O God, help me gladly to receive and obey this Thy word.

O God, once more I would recall in Thy presence, my fellow Christians everywhere . . . and in particular, those I know so well at my local church.

I think first of the minister of my church . . . who has a more difficult task to perform than often I realise . . . whose calling it is to preach the Gospel, making it clear to people such as me . . . to teach the meaning of the Bible, and the Christian faith . . . to speak the truth in love at all times, without fear or favour.

O God, grant Thy rich blessing upon the minister of my church, those who are dear to him; and to all other preachers of the Gospel whom I may know. Amen.

I think of those with whom I regularly share fellowship at my church . . . the leaders and members of the Youth Fellowship or whatever meeting I attend . . . and the members of my youth organisation who may not attend any meeting for direct Christian training and fellowship. . . .

O God, give to us who call ourselves Christian, a true desire to share the good news we have received, with other people, whether young or old. I pray Thy blessing upon our fellowship meeting in which we seek to understand Thy Book and Thy ways. Grant that as we enter into larger groups, even within the fellowship of our local church, in which there are those who have yet to commit their way to Thee, we may bear witness which is attractive and faithful. For Christ's sake. Amen.

I think of some of the older people at my church . . . for some of whom I have great respect, and some of whom I find it hard at times to like or understand. . . .

O God, help both the younger and older people at my church to understand each other. Help us to be sensitive and patient and keep us from those breaches of good manners and Christian courtesy which break Christian fellowship. I pray Thy strength and blessing upon elderly members of my church; those who through age and infirmity cannot share the work, fellowship and Sunday worship as they once did. Help those of us who are younger to do all in our power to strengthen fellowship with them and all others who are older than we are. Make us strong to think and believe the best about older folk, slow to criticise, swift and constant in friendliness.

Jesus said : I, if I be lifted up, will draw all men unto me.

I think now of my fellow Christians all over the world.

I marvel as I dwell upon the fact that Jesus Christ is Lord of all, King of all earthly kings, and has drawn men from hundreds of nations to Him in loyalty and obedience.

My faith is not narrow, exclusive, nationalistic. It is neither a product of my native country nor culture. It is not for some people only. It is for all men, everywhere. It is the truth. It is the message of God's unchanging, universal, eternal goodwill to mankind, made known in Jesus Christ.

I praise Thee, O Father, that I am permitted to share in the glad good news of Thy Gospel. I wonder at the way in which Christ has revealed Thee as Redeemer and Lord, to the communities of the world. I give Thee thanks for Christians of other races about whom I have known or read; for the fellowship which binds us together and makes us all one in Christ Jesus.

I thank Thee for those, who, over the centuries, counted their lives cheap for the sake of the Gospel; and leaving home and kindred, ventured far and wide to share Thy truth with others. I remember how they brought healing, enlightenment, hope, to dark and squalid places. I remember how they were instrumental in releasing men and women from the awful tyranny of devilish custom and primitive superstition: and how in every land the truth of Christ has meant added wellbeing and true enlightenment for those who were struggling after freedom and truth. I recall how that selfsame work still proceeds even until this very day; that even as I pray, devoted men and women are giving their all for the sake of others, in countries far and near.

I pray for these my fellow disciples. Some of them are enduring far harder things for the Gospel's sake than any I have so far met, or am likely to meet.

Lord, let me not live ignorant of and indifferent to these other members of the family of Christ. Stir up continually within me a real, sustained desire to gain more knowledge of them, that I may enter sympathetically into their experience, and be the more ready and able to interpret the faith to those about me. Amen.

*In my Father's house are many abiding places; if it were
not so, I would have told you: for I go to prepare a
place for you. And if I go to prepare a place for you,
I come again, and will receive you unto myself; that
where I am, there ye may be also.*

*If in this life only we have hoped in Christ, we are of
all men most pitiable.*

*For none of us liveth to himself, and none dieth to
himself.*

*For whether we live, we live unto the Lord; or whether
we die, we die unto the Lord: whether we live therefore,
or die, we are the Lord's.*

To die is as natural as to be born. One day I, too, shall
die. The ending of life here on earth will come. I
shall have done with this body of mine, which looks so
solid and enduring, and of which I am secretly tempted
to be proud.

When that moment comes, what shall I still have left?
A spirit gloriously alive to God. . . ?

The humble hope of hearing the Master's "Well
done . . ."?

Am I afraid to think about death?

O God, I would be neither morbid nor flippant about
this matter. Rather would I face it reverently and
sensibly, as befits a child of Thine whose faith, now and
in the world to come, is in Thyself.

O God, I pray Thee to prevent me from becoming
disturbed and distressed about the fact of life's earthly
closing. I know my sense of helplessness and aversion
in the presence of strange and awesome things. Thou
hast mercifully veiled from our eyes the sight of the
heavenly places. But nothing in life or death can take
Thy children from the reach of Thy care. Then, O
Father, grant me that sure trust in Thee, that the childish
fears which might threaten me may be swept away,
and that I may live my days in the knowledge of Thy
presence and safekeeping.

But if I sometimes fear to die because in my heart
I know I should be ashamed to give an account of myself
before Thee, then, O Lord, quicken within me a truer
devotion to Thyself. Prevent me from that carelessness
and disobedience which can quench within me the sense
of Thy calling and the desire to fulfil it. Amen.

Father of all mercies, I worship Thee with a thankful heart. Again today Thy guiding hand will be over me. I shall share in the bustling traffic of life. Now for a short while, I would pray Thee to break to me the Bread of Life, that I may go in the strength of it. May I live this day confidently aware of Thy presence, Thy blessing upon my life.

I would say my prayers for those in special need.

For those who this day will have prized hopes shattered:
Lord, hear my prayer.
For those likely to be overwhelmed by sudden sharp temptations:
Lord, hear my prayer.
For those finding it desperately hard to exercise self-control:
Lord, hear my prayer.
For those sorely tempted to harbour strong contempt towards one another:
Lord, hear my prayer.
For those just estranged from their loved ones, and wanting reconciliation:
Lord, hear my prayer.
For those living under suspicion:
Lord, hear my prayer.
For those who have suffered failure after failure:
Lord, hear my prayer.
For those in pain:
Lord, hear my prayer.
For those who are lonely, and forsaken:
Lord, hear my prayer.
For those who are sick at heart:
Lord, hear my prayer.

He that dwelleth in the secret place of the Most High shall abide under the shadow of the Almighty. I will say of the Lord, He is my refuge and my fortress; my God, in whom I trust, for thou, O Lord, art my refuge! Because he hath set his love upon me, therefore will I deliver him: I will set him on high, because he hath known my name. He shall call upon me, and I will answer him; I will be with him in trouble: I will deliver him and honour him. With long life will I satisfy him, and shew him my salvation.

Lord, I have called upon thee; make haste unto me:
Give ear unto my voice, when I call unto Thee.
Let my prayer be set forth as incense before thee;
The lifting up of my hands as the evening sacrifice.
Set a watch, O Lord, before my mouth;
Keep the door of my lips.

Lord, I am thankful that there need be placed no restraint upon the door of my lips as I offer my praise and worship for all Thou hast done, in Jesus Christ, for mankind and me.

> *Jesus! the name that charms our fears,*
> *That bids our sorrows cease;*
> *'Tis music in the sinner's ears,*
> *'Tis life, and health and peace.*

Lord, even as I gratefully recollect Thy mighty acts wrought in Jesus Christ, I pray for those who are dead to Thee; those who sorrow blindly without hope of Thy comfort; those who are in bondage to their own desires, and know nothing of Christian liberty.

Thy kingdom come, Thy will be done, in earth as it is in heaven.

I thank Thee, O Father, that Thou hast always put into the hearts of men a great desire and longing for the day to dawn when they shall live, inarmed, as brothers; for the establishment of Thy kingly reign of peace and righteousness, when fear, cruelty, hatred and oppression shall have been destroyed through the power of Christ. I pray for all who consciously work and strive for Thy kingdom's coming.

For those who speak the truth in love.
For those who write words of wisdom and challenge.
For those who plan changes in the affairs of men to bring added happiness.
For those Thou hast permitted to hold great power over their fellows.

Prevent me ever, O Lord, from thinking that only such folk as these for whom I have prayed can do the effective work of Thy kingdom. Rather do Thou help me continually to believe and know that the countless unremembered acts of love and service, goodness and truth, by Thy people everywhere, are the true foundations of the City, whose builder and maker is God.

*He giveth power to the faint: and to him that hath no
might he increaseth strength . . . they that wait upon
the Lord shall renew their strength; they shall mount up
with wings as eagles. . . .*
God so loved that He gave. . . .
God, who giveth us richly all things to enjoy. . . .

O Lord, let me not soil this clean new day by living
mean and grudgingly. Give me Thy divinely generous
spirit to instruct my mind and warm my heart. Help
me to be greathearted in my dealings with others, looking
for the very best in them, offering myself freely to them.
Let no cold or sullen words pass my lips. Let my
appearance be such as to encourage friendship, not check
its approach. Restrain me from all littlemindedness, back-
biting, hardness of heart and unwillingness to forgive.

*Lord only Thou canst enable me to live as in my
best moments I know I was born to live; forgetting
myself, cleaving to Christ, rejoicing to serve Him with
singlehearted zeal. I pray Thee now to forgive my selfishness, to root it from my life, to help me grow in the
grace of my Lord Jesus Christ from day to day.*

As I think about my need to lose sight of self, let
me ponder for a moment about my spending habits . . .
remembering that money is such a significant symbol for
so many people. . . .
What money has been mine to use this last week?
How much have I willingly handed to others . . . to
God, in church, last Sunday . . . to my parents,
guardians, or friends . . . to any good cause. . . ?
How much have I spent on myself . . . on sweets . . .
cigarettes . . . films . . . outings . . . luxuries?
What have I saved. . . ?
Am I able to face God with this testimony without
shame?

O God, grant me to hate being niggardly with others
alike as with Thee. Thou hast given everything for me.
I worship Thee in the name of One Who joyously counted
nothing as a prize save the doing of Thy good and
perfect will; One Who had no thought for petty pleasure
or self-indulgence.
Teach me how to throw my life and ambitions away
for the sake of Christ, that I may truly inherit the unending wealth of joy and fulfilment He has prepared for
all His disciples both now and in the world to come.

Have mercy upon me, O God, according to thy loving-kindness :
According to the multitude of thy tender mercies blot out my transgressions.
Wash me throughly from mine iniquity,
And cleanse me from my sin.
For I acknowledge my transgressions :
And my sin is ever before me.
Against thee, thee only, have I sinned,
And done that which is evil in thy sight :
That thou mayest be justified when thou speakest,
And be clear when thou judgest.
Hide thy face from my sins,
And blot out all my iniquities.
Create in me a clean heart, O God;
And renew a right spirit within me.
Cast me not away from thy presence;
And take not thy holy spirit from me.
Restore unto me the joy of thy salvation :
And uphold me with a free spirit.
Then will I teach transgressors thy ways;
And sinners shall be converted unto thee.
Deliver me from blood-guiltiness, O God, thou God of my salvation;
And my tongue shall sing aloud of thy righteousness.
O Lord, open thou my lips;
And my mouth shall shew forth thy praise.
For thou delightest not in sacrifice; else would I give it :
Thou hast no pleasure in burnt offering.
The sacrifices of God are a broken spirit :
A broken and a contrite heart, O God, thou wilt not despise.

O Christ, my Master, in Whose life courtesy and courage were equally yoked, I pray for Thy likeness to be found in me. Often I am tempted to be slack, insensitive, self-indulgent. I set great store by obvious virtues, and neglect the fine details of life and conduct which reveal the worth of a man.

I pray for the desire and ability to harness my whole life, in actions and attitudes great and small, to Thy will and purpose. In particular, I pray for good sense and resolution. . . .

To get up in decent time to say my prayers, and start the day without getting on people's nerves;

To give myself a clean and attractive appearance, without fuss or vanity;

To give my whole attention to those I am dealing with, and to avoid the appearance of offhandedness;

To make time for cheerfulness, instead of grousing;

To conquer any bashfulness I feel in going out of my way to help little children, old folk, infirm and blind people and anybody who obviously needs a helping hand;

To voice swiftly my appreciation of kindnesses received, and never rudely to take even the smallest kindness for granted;

To honour constantly my simple code of good manners;

To replace idle gossip and cynical comment with decent conversation;

To take care my preferences in radio programmes and the rest aren't forced on my family and friends to their discomfort and irritation;

To laugh at myself sometimes;

To make a deliberate effort to see myself as others see me, and to try sincerely by God's help to amend those faults and failings which are an offence to others.

O God, as this day I go about my business, I would bear about with me the marks of the Lord Jesus. Help me to be increasingly aware that it is the little things which do indeed count, and which build up the picture of myself I have so long been giving to those around me. My non-Christian companions are reading the gospel according to me.

Lord, I believe. Help Thou my unbelief. Amen.

Once again, the work of the day is done. Its moments are fled, and in the quietness of this time and place I give my mind to God. Throughout the day He has silently stood by me; He has been the unseen listener to my conversation, has seen my acts, has known my thoughts.

Let me gladly recollect, in God's sight, everything of good this day has brought, giving thanks for His loving-kindness which has been round about me. Let me ask for grace, truly to repent of sins in word, thought, or deed, which this day I have committed. . . . Let me be bold to ask for the continuing grace of God to upbuild within me the strength and winsomeness of the faithful Christian.

O God, I crave the gift of wisdom.

Often I am perplexed. I do not know how to choose aright. Often I see how I should have acted when it is too late. I cannot easily discern between the glittering attractions of life, and the things which are of real worth. Bestow upon me, I pray, the power to look into the heart of things.

O God, I crave the gift of power to persevere.

I easily grow weary in welldoing. I remember Jesus said that those who endured to the end should be saved. But I am tempted to give up when things go hard with me, and to be overwhelmed by disappointment. Thou, Lord, only canst make up in me what is lacking. Grant me to be a good soldier of Jesus, enduring hardness and abiding faithful.

O God, I crave the gift of singleheartedness.

I am sometimes troubled to find that I am serving Thee because others will think well of me, or because it pleases me to do so; not simply because I love Thee. Give me purity of intention, I pray. Help me to see wherein my motives are mixed, and recognise quickly when love for Thee and love of self confuse my mind.

O Lord, these are not the only gifts of Thy love for which I would pray. I need courage, tolerance, under-standing, cheerfulness, modesty and all the other pure and wholesome virtues which are the fruits of the Holy Spirit. Only as Thou dost indwell me can I find them springing to birth within my life.

*Have this mind in you, which was also in Christ Jesus:
Who, being in the form of God, counted it not a prize
to be on an equality with God,
But emptied himself, taking the form of a servant, being
made in the likeness of men;
And being found in fashion as a man, he humbled himself, becoming obedient even unto death, yea, the death
of the cross.*

And they bring him unto the place Golgotha, which
is, being interpreted, The place of the skull.

And they crucify him, and part his garments among
them, casting lots upon them, what each should take.

And the superscription of his accusation was written
over, THE KING OF THE JEWS.

*He was despised and rejected of men; a man of sorrows,
and acquainted with grief: and as one from whom men
hide their face he was despised, and we esteemed him not.
Surely he hath borne our sickness and carried our
sorrows: yet we did esteem him stricken, smitten of God,
and afflicted.
But he was wounded for our transgressions, he was
bruised for our iniquities: the chastisement of our peace
was upon him; and with his stripes we are healed.
All we like sheep have gone astray; we have turned
every one to his own way; and the Lord hath laid on
him the iniquity of us all.*

> *O Love divine! what hast Thou done?*
> *The immortal God hath died for me!*
> *The Father's co-eternal Son*
> *Bore all my sins upon the tree:*
> *The immortal God for me hath died!*
> *My Lord, my Love is crucified.*

*By Thy Cross and Passion, O Saviour Christ, Thou
hast set forever forth for all men the clear and shining
evidence of Thy inexhaustible love. And by that same
Cross is made dreadfully plain, the fell and hideous
power of sin. O grant that as I dare to look at the
Cross with eyes of faith and adoration, I may receive
pardon for my sins, newness of life, and the assurance of
Thy ever-present power to keep me from falling; through
Thy redeeming blood. Amen.*

*I began this day by thinking of the Cross of Christ. I
would now ask God to help me see the inwardness of
this great hymn of Christian experience, that the saving
knowledge of Christ, of which it triumphantly sings, may
be mine.*

> And can it be that I should gain
>   An interest in the Saviour's blood?
> Died He for me, who caused His pain?
>   For me, who Him to death pursued?
> Amazing love! how can it be
> That Thou, my God, shouldst die for me!
>
> 'Tis mystery all! The Immortal dies :
>   Who can explore His strange design?
> In vain the first-born seraph tries
>   To sound the depths of love divine.
> 'Tis mercy all! let earth adore,
> Let angel minds inquire no more.
>
> He left His Father's throne above—
>   So free, so infinite His grace—
> Emptied Himself of all but love,
>   And bled for Adam's helpless race.
> 'Tis mercy all, immense and free;
> For, O my God, it found out me!
>
> Long my imprisoned spirit lay
>   Fast bound in sin and nature's night;
> Thine eye diffused a quickening ray—
>   I woke, the dungeon flamed with light;
> My chains fell off, my heart was free,
> I rose, went forth, and followed Thee.
>
> No condemnation now I dread;
>   Jesus, and all in Him, is mine!
> Alive in Him, my living Head,
>   And clothed in righteousness divine,
> Bold I approach the eternal throne,
> And claim the crown, through Christ, my own.

Lord, I would thank Thee for two things; for the daily round and common task of ordinary expected things: and for the out-of-the-ordinary experiences which sometimes come my way; when I am strongly conscious of another world, out of space and time.

I think now with warmed heart and mind upon the memory of such moments.

For untainted joy in the company of a loved one;
For sheer enchantment and awe in the presence of some brilliantly gifted performer;
For the delight found in timeless beauty within the worlds of nature and art and science;
For writings of varied kinds which held me enthralled;

I praise Thy holy name, O Father Eternal

In these moments my heart and mind were both held prisoner. I forgot myself. I had to 'come back to earth' again from the strangely beautiful, strangely familiar heaven into which I had been permitted to enter for a brief space.

Yet, in remembering these times of vision and rapture, I would not be so stupid as to turn away discontented today from the daily round and common task. I could never know the wonder of the exceptional unless I was accustomed to the ordinary.

Teach me, then, O God, to live my days thankful too for the life of every day with its healthful work, its dependable order and regularity.

I would pray for:

All blind and dumb people:
All those whose bodies have been cruelly disfigured or mutilated in war and accident, and who must lie helpless, often in pain, and out of sight and sound of their loved ones:
All those who are sick in mind, unable to think, speak and behave like ordinary people.

O God, the strength of the weak, the comfort oᴸ the lonely, the deliverer of those who despair, I pray Thine especial blessing upon all these my brothers and sisters, children of Thine. It is only by good fortune that I am not among their number. Prevent me from becoming so absorbed in my own joys, and in the life of the world about me, that these Thy needy ones are forgotten. Amen.

Our Lord spoke to His disciples, and said:

Come ye after me, and I will make you fishers of men.
Lord Jesus, I would hear Thee speak this word to me.

Abide in me, and I in you. As the branch cannot bear fruit of itself, except it abide in the vine; so neither can ye, except ye abide in me.
Lord Jesus, I would hear Thee speak this word to me.

But when they deliver you up, be not anxious how or what ye shall speak: for it shall be given you in that hour what ye shall speak.
Lord Jesus, I would hear Thee speak this word to me.

Whosoever would become great among you shall be your minister; and whosoever would be first among you shall be your servant: even as the Son of man came not to be ministered unto, but to minister, and to give his life a ransom for many.
Lord Jesus, I would hear Thee speak this word to me.

If any man would come after me, let him deny himself, and take up his cross daily, and follow me.
For whosoever would save his life shall lose it; but whosoever shall lose his life for my sake, the same shall save it.
Lord Jesus, I would hear Thee speak this word to me.

Go ye into all the world and preach the gospel to the whole creation.
Lord Jesus, I would hear Thee speak this word to me.

The harvest truly is plenteous, but the labourers are few.
Pray ye therefore the Lord of the harvest, that he send forth labourers into his harvest.
Lord Jesus, I would hear Thee speak this word to me.

Ask, and it shall be given you; seek, and ye shall find; knock, and it shall be opened unto you.
For everyone that asketh receiveth; and he that seeketh findeth; and to him that knocketh it shall be opened.

These things have I spoken unto you, that my joy may be in you, and that your joy may be fulfilled.
Lo, I am with you alway, even unto the end of the world.
Even so, come, Lord Jesus.

O Lord, our Lord, how excellent is thy name in all the earth! who hast set thy glory upon the heavens.

When I consider thy heavens, the work of thy fingers, the moon and the stars, which thou hast ordained;

What is man, that thou art mindful of him? and the son of man, that thou visitest him?

Lord God, Thou hast set me to live my days in a world of unending variety, wealth, beauty, mystery. Prevent me, I pray, from ever becoming so full of my own conceit that I cease to wonder at the marvels of Thy handiwork. I understand a little of the countless wonders of scientific discovery. Forgive me if ever I yield to the absurd temptation to think I know everything, and treat others as if they knew nothing; especially older folk, far wiser than I in their knowledge of Thee, their fellowmen, and life itself. When I am tempted to impress people by airing the bit of knowledge others have laboriously taught me, save me from making a fool of myself. Teach me more and more the secret of true humility, and the art of learning from everyone around me.

Lord, I worship Thee as Lord and Giver of Life, as I ponder on:

The mystery of the myriad stars in their appointed courses.
The incredible ingenuity of machinery.
The marvel of human speech, and writing.
The discoveries of modern medicine and surgery.
The flawless goodness of my Lord Christ.

O Lord, I would pray at this moment for those who are tired of life because they are wrapped up in themselves; for those who are not treading the highway of Christian life, but going round in dreary circles of petty pleasure. I pray for those who are desperately bored and discontented, who feel that life has cheated them of its true radiance and glory.

I pray for those who, perhaps through no fault of their own, have never been helped to look around them with awe and wonder, but only with fear and suspicion, or a hard and calculating stare. Lord, grant that I at least may so live this day that such people might find something in my life to remind them of eternal truth and beauty, and of Thee, the Author of Goodness. Amen.

*I bow my knees unto the Father, from whom every
family in heaven and on earth is named. . . . He made
of one every nation of men for to dwell on all the face
of the earth. . . .
For ye are all sons of God; through faith, in Jesus Christ.
There can be neither Jew nor Greek, bond nor free, there
can be no male and female: for ye all are one man in
Christ Jesus.*

I come into the presence of God, recalling tonight
especially the cruel tensions of the world I live in. I
remember the selfishness, fear, and misunderstanding
which have thrown up monstrous barriers between white
men and coloured peoples in so many countries throughout the world.
I remember the deeply embedded suspicions and
animosity of west towards east, east towards west: the
solid distrust of motives on each side.
I remember the awful, growing hatred and envy of the
dispossessed, backward people of the earth, towards
those who have seemingly expropriated and beggared
them; and the unreasoning obstinacy and hardness of
heart of some who hold the reins of power over their
fellows.

Speed the day, O Lord God, when false idols of race
and blood, false gospels of hatred and conflict, shall be
uprooted and destroyed.
Help us never to grow weary in well-doing, dis-
heartened because the fight against selfishness, injustice,
and human wrong in its myriad forms drags wearily on
and spectacular victories hardly ever happen. Help us to
remember the Cross of Christ.

Hear me good Lord as I pray:
    For those who this night burn with resentment against
their fellowmen.
    For those who are the unhappy victims of unreasoned
fear and prejudice.
    For those who have deliberately chosen to embrace lies
about their fellowmen, preferring them to the truth.
    For those who live in a black night of despair and
terror through the sin of others; those who are without
liberty; those who are without hope.

O Christ, hear my prayer for all such.

But on the first day of the week, at early dawn, they
came unto the tomb . . . and found the stone rolled
away . . . and it came to pass while they were perplexed
thereabout, behold two men stood by them in dazzling
apparel . . . and they said unto them, why seek ye, the
living among the dead?   He is not here, but is risen. . . .

> *This is the day the Lord hath made,*
> *That all may see His love displayed,*
> *May feel His resurrection's power,*
> *And rise again to fall no more,*
> *In perfect righteousness renewed,*
> *And filled with all the life of God.*

Then, O Father, let me live this day joyously aware
that Christ is risen indeed.   Let me worship Thee gladly
and reverently, with a sense of home-coming as I enter
Thy house.

I thank Thee for the inheritance into which I have
entered, of a Christian Sunday which I may use freely to
Thy glory, without any restraint or fear.   Teach me to
resist firmly and courteously all which would cheapen
this hallowed day.

At worship today, and in the name of my fellow-
Christians, as for myself, I pray:

For the gifts of reverence, understanding and faithful
expectancy.

For freedom from inattention, distracting thoughts and
impulses.

For the desire to be truly obedient to Thy holy word.

For the ability to resist all temptation to foolish or
uncharitable criticism of the preacher or his message.

I pray:

For those who will conduct worship at my church
today. . . .

For all Christian preachers everywhere; especially those
in strange and difficult surroundings.

For all church musicians.

For sidesmen and all others in whose hands rests the
good name of the Church.

For all those who will teach or share in Sunday
Schools, Youth Fellowships, and all other groups.

Lord, may this Sunday be a day on which great things
are attempted for Thee.   Grant me to have a part in
them.   For Thy Name's sake.   Amen.

At the ending of the first Resurrection day, Christ made Himself known to the disciples . . . they became gloriously aware that He had conquered . . . they became changed people. . . .

Come, then, Lord Jesus, I ask Thee, and make me deeply conscious of Thy presence and power at the close of this Thy day.

Let me first remember how I have spent this Sunday:
At worship . . . and in fellowship. . . .
What have I freshly learned today about the faith of a Christian? . . .
What was the preacher's message? . . .
What hymns and prayers and Bible readings spoke new truths, disclosed new horizons, to me? . . .
How much real attention did I pay? How much real concentration of mind and soul did I offer? . . .

What else have I done today?
This day, like all before it, God gave me to use to His glory, and so to my true enjoyment. Could I offer it back to Him now, without shame? Then let me do so.

Lord I pray:

For those who have committed their lives to Christ for the first time today; that they may grow sturdily in Christian faith and experience. . . .
For those who are now pondering what they have heard of Thee today, and are not far from Thy Kingdom; that they may receive the strength they need. . . .
For those who are fighting against Thy call, which they know they should obey; that the victory may be Thine. . . .
For those whose love and loyalty to Thee has weakened, and who despise themselves for it; that they may make a fresh start. . . .
For those who are tired from a day's strenuous pleasure-seeking, and depressed because they are dissatisfied at heart; that their eyes may be opened to Thee.

And now, O Father, into Thy care I commit this night all these Thy children whom I have remembered before Thee: all distressed and unhappy people: the sick and lonely: my loved ones, near or far away; especially
. . . .
For the love of Christ and for His sake. Amen.